KENT ARCHAEOLOGICAL SOCIETY

KENT RECORDS

VOLUME XXVI

1997

The beginning of the record of the trials in Archbishop Warham's register (fo. 159R; actual size 17 in. × 13¼ in.; parchment)

KENT RECORDS

General Editor: A.P. Detsicas, B.A., M.A., D.Litt., F.S.A.

KENT HERESY
PROCEEDINGS 1511–12

Edited by

NORMAN TANNER

Published by the Kent Archaeological Society
The Museum
St. Faith's Street, Maidstone
Kent

1997

Produced for the Society by
Sutton Publishing Limited, Phoenix Mill, Thrupp, Stroud,
Gloucestershire GL5 2BU.
Printed in Great Britain by
Hartnolls, Bodmin, Cornwall

ISBN 0 906746 25 6

CONTENTS

v

ACKNOWLEDGEMENTS

The text and the frontispiece are published by permission of the Archbishop of Canterbury and the Trustees of Lambeth Palace Library. I am most grateful for the help given by Ms Melanie Barber, Deputy Librarian and Archivist of the Library.

Christopher Saxton's map of 1575, used for the dust-jacket, is by permission of the British Library (Maps C.7.c.l. Saxton).

I thank the Kent Archaeological Society for undertaking the publication and Dr A. Detsicas, Honorary Editor of the Society, for his support; Sutton Publishing; Angela and Gerard Waghorn for hospitality; Margaret Aston, Andrew Hope and Anne Hudson for their help.

Publication has been made possible by generous grants from the British Academy, the Scouloudi Foundation and the Society of Jesus.

NORMAN TANNER,
CAMPION HALL, OXFORD

ABBREVIATIONS

BRUC	A.B. Emden, *A Biographical Register of the University of Cambridge to 1500* (Cambridge, 1963)
BRUO	A.B. Emden, *A Biographical Register of the University of Oxford to A.D. 1500* (3 vols., Oxford, 1957–9)
Churchill, *Canterbury Administration*	I.J. Churchill, *Canterbury Administration* (2 vols., London, 1933)
Foxe, *Acts* (Ed. Pratt)	John Foxe, *Acts and Monuments* (Ed. J. Pratt, 8 vols., London, 1877)
Hudson, *Premature Reformation*	A. Hudson, *The Premature Reformation: Wycliffite Texts and Lollard History* (Oxford, 1988)
Kentish Visitations	(Ed.) K.L. Wood-Legh, *Kentish Visitations of Archbishop William Warham and his Deputies, 1511–12*, Kent Records, xxiv (1984)
Norwich Trials	(Ed.) N.P. Tanner, *Heresy Trials in the Diocese of Norwich, 1428–31*, Camden 4th series, xx (1977)
Thomson, *Later Lollards*	J.A.F. Thomson, *The Later Lollards, 1414–1520* (Oxford, 1965)
Woodcock, *Canterbury*	B.L. Woodcock, *Medieval Ecclesiastical Courts in the Diocese of Canterbury* (London, 1952)

INTRODUCTION

The present proceedings, which are contained in fos. 159r–175v of the register of Archbishop Warham of Canterbury, are one of the most informative records of Lollard trials in England on the eve of the Reformation, certainly the fullest from Kent. Fifty-three suspects[1] from the diocese were brought before the archbishop between April 1511 and June 1512. The large majority of them abjured their errors. Most of the abjurations were recorded in full, together with the penances imposed, which were very detailed. Five of the accused, however, refused to abjure and were condemned as relapsed or obdurate heretics. In these five cases the depositions of witnesses were recorded and they provide further information about the organisation and dissemination of Lollardy in the area.

The parts recorded in English, especially the depositions, are of interest both generally as examples of the language in the early sixteenth century and more specifically as providing information about the use of the vernacular in Lollardy.

The proceedings were cited and commented upon at length, though not always accurately, by John Foxe.[2] Long extracts, amounting to about a third of the total material, were printed in the last century by S.R. Maitland.[3] John Thomson and Anne Hudson, among recent writers, have discussed the evidence in some detail.[4] The complete text, however, has not been edited previously.

The present work complements, I hope, Kathleen Wood-Legh's edition of the visitations of parishes and religious houses conducted by Archbishop Warham and his deputies in the years 1511–12, which was published by the Kent Archaeological Society in 1984.[5]

---

[1] See Table 1.

[2] Foxe, *Acts* (Ed. Pratt), iv, 181–2 and 722–3, and v, 647–54.

[3] S.R. Maitland, 'Persecution in Kent', *British Magazine and monthly register of religious and ecclesiastical information, parochial history . . .*, xxiii (January to June, 1843), 393–402 and 629–33, xxiv (July to December, 1843), 133–8, 256–9 and 638–43, and xxv (January to June, 1844), 141–5. I am indebted to Mr Andrew Hope for drawing my attention to this work.

[4] Thomson, *Later Lollards*, 183–90; Hudson, *Premature Reformation*, 134–6, 143, 150–1 and 156.

[5] *Kentish Visitations* (as under 'Abbreviations').

i. The manuscript and its contents

The folios in question run 159 to 167, 167*, 168 to 175 in Warham's register.[6] They, together with fo. 176 which is blank, form two quires of the register. The writing is in a single, clear and elegant, early six-teenth-century hand. The name of the scribe is not known.[7] The writing is continuous throughout, without any gaps or blank folios apart from the final one. All the material in the two quires relates to the proceedings, there is nothing extraneous.

The quires form a fair copy written up from earlier drafts. This conclusion seems certain both from the neat and continuous presentation, just mentioned, and from the fact that the proceedings do not follow in chronological order in the register. In this edition the sections have been arranged in chronological order, for the sake of convenience. Table 2 compares this sequence with that in the register. There is no apparent reason for the order in which the proceedings appear in the register.

The assumption must be, therefore, that notes were taken at the time of the proceedings and these were subsequently – probably fairly soon afterwards – written up into the present record. Later still, probably soon after Warham's death in 1532, the two quires were bound together with other quires to form the register, which at a subsequent re-binding was divided into two volumes. The folio numbers, which are also of a later date, continue through the two volumes.

The largest portion of the material consists of the abjurations of the defendants who submitted, which are recorded in full in most cases, and the penances imposed on them. Indeed, the initial heading of the record reads 'Nomina abiurationum . . . una cum actis abiurationum suarum' and the only other main heading, for the year 1512, describes the proceedings as 'Abiurationes'.[8] Another important part of the material consists of the proceedings against the five defendants who refused to retract. These proceedings are recorded very fully, including the depositions of witnesses. The relinquishments of the five persons to the secular arm were also recorded. The other material consists of a formula of absolution from excommunication, the dismissal of one suspect who was not convicted, and the oath of another to appear before the archbishop when summoned.

The abjurations and depositions are in English, almost all the remaining material is in Latin.

[6] The register is kept at Lambeth Palace Library, London. For a description of it see D.M. Smith, *Guide to Bishops' Registers of England and Wales* (London, 1981), 16–17.

[7] See also Churchill, *Canterbury Administration*, ii, 242 and below, xi–xii.

[8] See below, 25 and 116, and frontispiece.

ii. The Trials

Archbishop Warham's proceedings formed one of several major drives against Lollards in the years 1510 to 1512: those of Bishops Fitzjames of London in 1510–11 and Smith of Lincoln in 1511, for both of which we are largely dependent on Foxe's *Acts and Monuments*,[9] and that of Bishop Blyth of Coventry and Lichfield in 1511–12, which survives as Lichfield Court Book B/C/13.[10] Warham's proceedings must be seen against the background of these other prosecutions. In the diocese of Canterbury, however, there is remarkably little evidence of other judicial proceedings against Lollards during the archbishop's tenure of the see from 1504 to 1532.[11]

The first of Warham's proceedings took place on 28 April, 1511, and the last on 28 June, 1512: the large majority of them were concentrated in the five months between 28 April and 23 September, 1511. They were held in various places in the diocese of Canterbury and at the archbishop's palace at Lambeth in Surrey. The largest number were held at the archbishop's residence at Knole near Sevenoaks, a fair number at Lambeth palace, and the remainder variously in Canterbury cathedral, the archbishop's residences in Canterbury, Maidstone and Otford, the collegiate church of All Saints at Maidstone, and the parish church of Saltwood.

Robert Woodward, the commissary general of Archbishop Warham, conducted the proceedings in two cases and Cuthbert Tunstall, the future Bishop of Durham and of London, acting as the archbishop's chancellor, in another.[12] In all but these three cases, all of them relatively minor ones, the presiding figure and judge was the archbishop himself: the normal phrase being 'ipso reverendissimo patre pro tribunali iudicialiter sedente'. Indeed, the general impression is of the archbishop taking the initiative throughout the proceedings. Also attesting to the importance of the trials was the numerous and formidable team of clerics assisting him. They included frequently Woodward and Tunstall and John Thornden, the archbishop's suffragan bishop, and on occasions Bishops John Fisher of Rochester and Richard Nykke of Norwich and the dean of St. Paul's cathedral, John Colet. William Potkyn, David Cooper, Thomas Laurence and John Colman were named as public notaries, the last two of whom

---

[9] Thomson, *Later Lollards*, 87–8, 162 and 238; Foxe, *Acts* (Ed. Pratt), iv, 123–6, 173–82, 208 and 214–15.

[10] J. Fines, 'Heresy Trials in the Diocese of Coventry and Lichfield, 1511–12', *Journal of Ecclesiastical History*, xiv (1963), 160–74; I. Luxton, 'The Lichfield Court Book: a Postscript', *Bulletin of the Institute of Historical Research*, xliv (1971), 120–5.

[11] Thomson, *Later Lollards*, 184–5 and 190.

[12] See below, 59, 113 and 124.

were also described as scribes,[13] and presumably the four men were responsible for recording the proceedings, either writing the records themselves or supervising others to do it.[14]

The proceedings partly overlapped in time the visitations of parishes and religious houses conducted by the archbishop and his deputies between September 1511 and November 1512, mentioned above, but there was a clear distinction of business. Whereas the proceedings appear to have been concerned exclusively with heresy, in the records of the visitations explicit references to the subject are few and brief.[15]

iii. The charges and the defendants' beliefs

A list of fourteen questions was presented to Robert Harryson, the first suspect to be tried. After an inquiry about which diocese he belonged to, they touched on the seven sacraments in the order of eucharist, baptism and confirmation, penance, priesthood, marriage and last anointing, followed by images, pilgrimages, prayers to saints, blessed bread and holy water. The final three questions concerned whether he still held any heretical opinions, whether any confession he might make would be genuine or fictitious, whether he had communicated with other heretics or possessed heretical books.[16] Harryson denied all the charges except that of belonging to the diocese of Canterbury and therefore of being subject to the archbishop's jurisdiction. Subsequently, he was condemned as an impenitent heretic. A virtually identical list of questions was presented to the other four defendants who were condemned as impenitent or relapsed heretics: William Carder, Agnes Grebill, John Browne and Edward Walker.

It seems likely that the same, or a similar, questionnaire was used in the other proceedings, though in these cases the questions were not recorded and must be deduced from the articles of heresy that the defendants abjured. The abjurations of forty-six persons were recorded: Table 3 lists the topics mentioned in them.

The eucharist was the most prominent topic inasmuch as it appears in the large majority of abjurations and almost invariably it was mentioned first. The issue was the real presence: whether only bread is present, not the body of Christ, 'flesh and blood', or, as in two instances,[17] 'God's body'. In one case the argument was added 'that God

[13] See below, 60.
[14] See Woodcock, Canterbury, 38–40, 112 and 120–1.
[15] Kentish Visitations, xv, xix, 40, 72, 207 and 209.
[16] See below, 2–3.
[17] See below 77 and 79.

made man but man cowde not make Gode.'[18] It is noticeable, however, that the word 'transubstantiation' was never used.

All six other sacraments featured. Baptism, confirmation and last anointing, called 'aneylyng', were said to be neither necessary nor profitable for a person's soul. With marriage the point at issue was the solemnisation of the sacrament, that is, the service in church. With penance the heretical opinion was that confession of sins ought not to be made to a priest; 'for it should be made only to God,' was an explanation sometimes added.[19] 'That there is no more power given by God to a priest than to a layman' was the heretical opinion concerning the sacrament of orders, and in the cases of the five persons condemned as obdurate or relapsed heretics the statement was expanded with the clauses 'in ministering the church's sacraments, celebrating masses or performing other sacred functions.'[20]

Pilgrimages were attacked for being 'not profitable neither meritorious for man's soul', labour and money spent in them was lost and in vain. Iconophobia expressed itself in the prohibition against worshipping crucifixes, or images of St. Mary and other saints, or making offerings to them; for images of saints are but 'stokks and stones', reads one abjuration.[21] In the longer charges against the five individuals who did not abjure, the language was stronger: both making pilgrimages and venerating images were called idolatrous practices. Prayers were to be addressed only to God, not to saints. Finally, bread and water were said to be no better after a priest's blessing than before it.

There were two unusual opinions, both concerning the human nature of Jesus Christ and each of them alleged against only one person. Simon Piers confessed to having believed that Christ was incarnate man at the beginning of the world, before his conception through Mary.[22] It was the only charge against him that was mentioned. John Bukherst, on the other hand, underplayed the humanity of Christ, believing that he was not incarnate or born of Mary, did not suffer for our redemption or rise on the third day.[23] In his case other charges were mentioned.

The picture of the defendants' beliefs that can be inferred from the abjurations is limited. The use of a fairly short questionnaire inevitably presents them in a stereotyped and summary fashion. If the defendants

---

[18] See below, 65.
[19] See below, 65 and 79.
[20] See below, 2, 9, 17, 44 and 51.
[21] See below, 108.
[22] See below, 59.
[23] See below, 117.

were asked about all the heresies mentioned in the questionnaire – though it cannot be regarded as certain that they were – those they denied holding may be inferred from their omission from the abjurations. On the other hand, the abjurations themselves speak of the heresies listed as being only a selection, or the more important, of those held by the abjurer. Indeed, the questionnaire was much narrower than some others, regarding both the number of topics covered and the detail included in them: those used, for example, by Bishops Polton of Worcester and Alnwick of Norwich in the early fifteenth century.[24] In short, the information comes to us largely through the eyes and according to the priorities of the prosecution, and Warham's first priority seems to have been to secure convictions on a relatively small number of charges where heresy was clear-cut, not to enter into the defendants' beliefs at all fully or sympathetically.

A few further insights into the defendants' beliefs emerge from the depositions against the five individuals who refused to retract. Regarding the eucharist, for example, the simple rejection of Christ's bodily presence to be found in the abjurations was nuanced by various deponents in the trial of Edward Walker: the eucharist is 'doon in a mynde to call people togider' and 'a thing made in mynde and for the remembraunce of Criste for the people, for Crists owne body was in heven and his worde was in erthe', and 'Crist hymself in his owne body gave brede to his disciples and not his owne body, and so doo preests in lykewise geve brede that cometh from God in remembraunce of the brede geven by Criste in his maundy.'[25] Agnes Grebill made various distinctions in her treatment of confession, according to her husband: 'she beleved that confession made to a preest beyng the folowar of Peter and beyng pure and clene in life was good and profitable, and no confession was good that was made to a preest not beyng of clene life, for he had no power to assoyle any man of his synnes.'[26] Rejection of pilgrimages was replaced, according to William Baker, a deponent at Edward Walker's trial, by giving money to a poor person.[27] William Baker also claimed that John Browne had denied the existence of purgatory, a belief that does not appear elsewhere in the proceedings.[28]

The extra information about the defendants' beliefs provided by the depositions is very restricted. This is not surprising inasmuch as the

---

[24] A. Hudson, 'The Examination of Lollards', *Bulletin of the Institute of Historical Research*, xlvi (1973), 145–59; *Norwich Trials*, 10–22, especially 19–20.
[25] See below, 52–4.
[26] See below, 14.
[27] See below, 53.
[28] See below, 46.

depositions were made in reply to the rather narrow questionnaire, so that any additional information spills out or is recorded almost by accident. Nevertheless, it is enough to suggest that the unorthodox beliefs of the defendants were wider in scope and more nuanced than the abjurations alone indicate. Allowing for the limitations of the evidence and its stereotyping effect, it seems reasonable nevertheless to locate the defendants within the mainstream of early sixteenth-century Lollardy, though it is noticeable that neither Lollardy nor John Wyclif are mentioned by name in the proceedings.

iv. The Sentences

The sentences, and the penances in them, are of considerable interest on account of their fullness and detail.

The five defendants who were condemned as relapsed or impenitent heretics, mentioned above, were handed over to the secular arm on the grounds that the church could do nothing more for them, in the knowledge that they would be burnt to death. The sentences were recorded in full as well as the relinquishments of the individuals to the secular arm.[29] The relinquishments were also recorded as significations of excommunication addressed to the crown by the archbishop.[30]

Of the other forty-eight suspects involved in the proceedings, penances were imposed on and recorded for forty-five of them.[31] In almost every case more than one penance was ordered, often half a dozen or so. Table 4 shows the frequency.

The most common penance was carrying a faggot on some public occasion. All thirty-three penitents who were given this penance were ordered to carry the faggot in their parish church on one or more Sundays and feast-days, usually beginning with the procession at the beginning of mass and then throughout the service itself. Many of them were told expressly to appear with feet and shins bare, and heads uncovered in the case of men, or clad only in their undergarments in the case of some women,[32] *more penitentis*. Some of them, in addition, were ordered a similar penitential ritual in other public places: the cathedral and market-place of Canterbury and the market-place of Cranbrook.[33]

---

[29] See below, 6–7, 14–15, 23–5, 49, and 57–8.

[30] Public Record Office, London, C/85/24, nos. 20–22 and 24–25.

[31] James Bukherst was dismissed as not convicted (see below, 123); William Bukherst was recorded only as taking an oath to appear before archbishop Warham when he was summoned (see below, 24); and in the case of Simon Piers his abjuration was recorded but no penance (see below, 59–60).

[32] 'induta sola camisia et uno lintheamine' (see below, 71 and 74), 'induta solomodo camisia et tunica, Anglice a kyrtell' (see below, 74).

[33] For Canterbury see below, 40, 71 and 74. For Cranbrook see 64.

With a similar symbolism, reminding the person of the penalty for relapsing into heresy, and also very public, was the wearing of a badge with a flaming faggot on it. The badge was to be clearly visible on the outer garment and worn in perpetuity, though with this penance the archbishop always mentioned explicitly the possibility of a dispensation from it some time in the future.

Many defendants were ordered not to move outside their parish or locality without obtaining the archbishop's permission or, in some cases, without informing him. The wording is usually somewhat imprecise, but it looks as though the prohibition normally concerned only a change of residence, though occasionally even temporary movements seem to have been forbidden.

Imprisonment within a religious house, which was the most severe penalty apart from capital punishment, was imposed, in order of the dates of their sentences, on Joan Olberde, John Grebill senior, Joan Lowes, Stephen Castelyn, Julian Hilles (probably), Robert Franke and William Pelland. With the possible exception of Julian Hilles they were to be imprisoned for life, though in most cases they were allowed a mile or two outside the religious house and the possibility of remission in the future was mentioned. All the houses lay within the diocese of Canterbury but some distance from the home of the individual in question; each person being assigned to a different house, women to nunneries and men to male communities.

Most of those sentenced to imprisonment were told to expect a diet of bread and water, though it seems probable that the intention was to confine this penance to Fridays. Two other people were ordered to abstain from fish on Fridays, one other from meat on Wednesdays.[34]

Restrictions in dress were imposed on six individuals, in addition to those who were ordered to dress penitentially while carrying a faggot. Five women were forbidden to wear a smock on Fridays,[35] and John Grebill senior to wear a linen under-garment (*camisia linea*) on Wednesdays and Fridays, for the rest of their lives.

Confession to a priest, reception of the eucharist, and the gruesome punishment of watching William Carder being burnt to death, were penances imposed on the first seven suspects who abjured.[36] None of these penances was repeated.

Other penances were: attendance at divine service in one's parish church on Sundays and feast-days, which was of course already an obligation for all Christians; recitation of the Lord's prayer, Hail Mary

---

[34] Margaret Baker and Joan Bukherst (Fridays), Joan Colyn (Wednesdays).
[35] Agnes Raynold, Alice Hilles, Joan Riche, Joan Lowes and Julian Hilles.
[36] See below, 36.

and creed; offering a candle. John Dodde was ordered to treat his wife well, no hint of a reason being given.

Finally, the obligations of informing the archbishop and his successors of any persons suspected of heresy and of any books belonging to such persons – duties that were also included in all the abjurations – as well as that of surrendering any heretical books that they themselves might possess, were mentioned as penances for many defendants.

The penances were among the most complex and detailed that are known of in trials of Lollards.[37] Warham, a canon lawyer by training and profession, appears to have taken considerable care in working them out. For the most part the penances were meant to speak for themselves inasmuch as they were very public and clear in their symbolism. Sometimes a more precise connection is apparent. Relinquishment to the secular arm, and subsequent death by burning, was the mandatory penalty for relapsed and obdurate heretics, according to the statute *De heretico comburendo* of 1401 and subsequent legislation;[38] and imprisonment seems to have been reserved, in the present proceedings, for defendants who had failed in their purgations or were heavily involved in Lollardy. Usually, though not always, those who abjured on the same day were given the same or similar penances. There may have been other reasons why certain penances were chosen for particular individuals but they are rarely apparent from the record of the proceedings. Women seem to have been treated in much the same way as men.

Little is known for certain about the performance of the penances. There is no record of the deaths of the five persons who were handed over to the secular arm, though the penance of having to watch the burning of William Carder suggests that the due process of law was indeed followed. The archbishop frequently mentioned the possibility that he or his successors might commute, mitigate or dispense from the penances imposed, so it may well be that the penitential discipline was considerably milder in practice than the sentences initially suggest.

v. The defendants and the practice of Lollardy

Some details about the fifty-three defendants are given in Table 4. As the Map (below, xxvi) shows, probably twenty-seven of them, just over half the total, came from Tenterden and the neighbouring villages of Benenden, Rolvenden, Cranbrook, Halden and Wittersham. Other clusters were eight from Maidstone and adjacent Boxley, Bearsted and East Farleigh; eight from Staplehurst; five from Ashford and adjacent

---

[37] For other trials see Thomson, *Later Lollards*, 231–6.
[38] *Ibid.*, 220–1.

Great Chart and Godmersham; four from Canterbury. They comprised seventeen women and thirty-six men. About half of them belonged to families with two or more suspects, usually husband and wife but sometimes including one or, in the case of the Grebill family, two siblings. Some of the families were related. Agnes Ive of Canterbury was the sister of Robert Hilles of Tenterden[39] and family links may be suspected between Vincent Lynche of Halden and John Lynche of Tenterden, Joan Riche of Wittersham and William Riche of Benenden, Joyce and John Bampton of Bearsted and Richard Bampton of Boxley.

The ages of fifteen defendants were mentioned, ranging from twenty to seventy-four: five in their twenties, all of whom were sons or daughters of other defendants; a thirty-three year old; one aged forty; seven in their sixties; one who was seventy-four. Altogether the impression is of a high median age and of a well established Lollard community.

All the suspects were lay men and women. The overall impression is of a predominantly artisan group of moderate wealth. None of them appears to have belonged to the gentry class or above. The occupations of ten men were mentioned: three cutlers, probably two weavers, a tailor, a fletcher, a shoemaker, a cordwainer, and a glover.[40] The only woman whose occupation was mentioned, Agnes Raynold, was described as a servant.

The depositions against Robert Harryson, William Carder, Agnes Grebill, John Browne and Edward Walker – the five defendants who refused to abjure – provide interesting information about the organisation and dissemination of Lollardy. While the abjurations of the other suspects speak generally of 'privy conventicles' and 'assemblies', and the teaching of errors and heresies, the depositions spell out what these gatherings and activities meant in practice.

The kinds and places of encounter varied, according to the recorded statements of the deponents. Robert Harryson expressed his beliefs to Christopher Grebill as they were 'goyng by the waye' between Great Chart and Benenden, and to William Riche at a fair at Tenterden on St. Mark's day.[41] William Carder taught Robert Hilles in the homes of both of them as well as at alehouses, in church and in 'other places'.[42] John Browne shared his thoughts with William Baker in a garden at Great Chart and while they 'walked by the waye' in Cranbrook parish.[43]

[39] See below, 12.
[40] For textile-workers of the region who were involved in Lollardy, see J.F. Davis, 'Lollard Survival and the Textile Industry in the South-east of England', *Studies in Church History*, iii (1966), 191–201.
[41] See below, 4–5.
[42] See below, 11.
[43] See below, 46.

The favoured place was the home. William Carder had taught John Grebill senior some twenty years earlier at Grebill's home in Tenterden, before the latter moved to neighbouring Benenden, while Grebill was 'werking in his lome': Carder 'began first to rede in a booke of ii evangelists and teche this deponent (Grebil) of the said his belyves'.[44] The context suggests that Carder was then a servant or employee of Grebill. Carder also 'commyned' with William Riche at the latter's house in Benenden.[45] Both depositions emphasised that nobody else was present at the meeting but larger gatherings were also mentioned. Agnes Ive and Elizabeth White visited Robert Harryson at his house in Canterbury and received instruction from him there.[46] John Browne stayed with Thomas Harwode and his wife Joan at their home in Rolvenden and they discussed their beliefs 'yn an evenyng sittyng by the fyre in the hall.' Joan and Thomas later reciprocated by visiting John Browne at his house in Ashford, where they continued their discussions 'sittyng all togider there by the fyre, etyng and drynkyng.'[47]

Several gatherings were mentioned at Edward Walker's house in Maidstone, the largest being the culmination of two days of meetings at the homes of various suspects. On the day after Christmas, probably in 1510, William Baker and John Bampton visited William Riche at his house in Benenden and spent the night there. Next day they all moved to John Bampton's house at Boxley (or nearby Otham), where they were joined by John's brother Richard and four other men and discussed together the doctrine of the eucharist. In the evening of that or the next day the whole party travelled to nearby Maidstone, where they were entertained at the home of Edward Walker and his wife. William Baker read aloud to the group 'a booke of Mathewe whereyn was conteyned the gospel in Englisshe' and they 'satt drynkyng' and discussing the eucharist and other sacraments. They were interrupted, however, by the arrival of two women, one of whom was described as 'the jaylors wife', upon which Edward Walker, not surprisingly 'beyng aferde to be suspected and espied,' bid the others depart: 'Sirs, drynke ye and make ye mery and high you from hens agayn!'[48]

The impression is of close but informal contacts, or contacts based on the everyday situations of life, rather than of more structured teaching. The depositions, however, also give the impression that most deponents wished to incriminate as few people as possible, so the gatherings may

---

[44] See below, 11.
[45] See below, 12.
[46] See below, 6.
[47] See below, 45–7.
[48] See below, 52–6, collating the several depositions.

well have been larger than the depositions suggest. That all the suspects were lay people, with no priests among them, provides a context.

The Grebills provide the best example of how beliefs were transmitted within a family. John Grebill senior's instruction from William Carder some twenty years earlier has been mentioned; he and his son Christopher said that Carder had taught them on various subsequent occasions. He said that his wife Agnes had originally been taught by himself and John Ive towards the end of King Edward IV's reign, that is, a decade earlier than his encounter with Carder. The instruction of the two sons, Christopher and John junior, aged twenty-two and twenty-one, respectively, at the time of the trials, had begun when they were aged about seven according to their father, rather later according to the sons. John senior said that he had taught them with the support of his wife Agnes and with the help of John Ive of Canterbury: an account with which the two sons agreed, though Christopher also mentioned the role of William Carder and both of them said they had accepted their parents' beliefs only shortly before the trials. The parents, however, seem to have been unsuccessful in converting their daughter inasmuch as a 'distrawght yong woman, doughter to the said John and Agnes Grebill' was mentioned in a context suggesting that she was unwilling to go along with her parents' views.[49]

Women comprised almost one in three of the defendants and many of them appear as committed Lollards with some wider influence. Their role in providing hospitality also seems to have been important. Nevertheless, the leading figures appear to have been, for the most part, men. Even in the Grebill family the initiatives seem to have come from John senior rather than from his wife Agnes, except of course in her refusal to abjure and her rejection of her husband's and sons' evidence.[50]

One leader stands out, William Carder. A weaver of Tenterden, the town from which the largest number of suspects came, many defendants attested to his seminal influence. His teaching of Robert Hilles and the Grebill family has been mentioned. Christopher Grebill said he 'hath been the myschief and destruccion of many men, by bringyng theym into the said mysbileves.' Agnes Ive, another deponent at his trial, said that her recently deceased husband John Ive, himself a teacher of Agnes Grebill back in Edward IV's reign, maintained that Carder was his 'techer and reder'. His links with the Ives, who lived in Canterbury, show his influence beyond the Tenterden area. Other deponents emphasised his importance. There may have been

---

[49] See below, 11–13 and 18–22. Christopher and John junior were described once as *filii naturales* of Agnes Grebill (18), but in other references to them the paternity of John senior is not called into question.

[50] See below, 18–22.

some piling the blame onto Carder in order to minimise the deponents' own responsibility, nevertheless his major influence seems clear.[51]

William Carder formed a link with a previous generation of Lollardy in Kent. According to John Grebill senior, he had said that his parents were 'of the same secte' and that his mother had fled from Tenterden about forty years earlier out of fear.[52] In other cases Lollard connections over a long time were revealed. John Ive had been a Lollard evangelist in Tenterden back in the 1480s, as mentioned, and presumably, too, at Canterbury while he lived there. John Browne's record of dissent stretched back to the fifteenth century. At his trial in 1511 he acknowledged that he had abjured various heresies before Cardinal Morton twelve years earlier and he said that he had learnt his errors originally from a certain John Riche, who, he thought, had been burnt at Halden in Kent.[53] John Bukherst of Staplehurst said he had held his dissenting beliefs for twelve years, Robert Bright of Maidstone for fourteen, John Baus of Boxley for sixteen, John Lynche of Tenterden for twenty, Rabage Benet of Staplehurst for twenty-three, 'and more' they all added.[54]

Indeed, it seems likely that there had been a continuous tradition of Lollardy in the region for a century or more. For the towns and villages from which the defendants came in 1511-12 were the same as, or close to, many of those that produced Lollards in the 1420s and 1430s; notably those who appear to have been associated with William White, the Lollard evangelist and one-time parish chaplain of Tenterden.[55] The geographical coincidence is remarkable, even though research until now has not been able to prove satisfactorily the links during the middle years of the fifteenth century.

Connections outside Kent and the diocese of Canterbury are more difficult to find. John Grebill senior admitted he did not know where William Carder's mother had fled to some forty years earlier, though moving out of the diocese would have made sense. He thought William Carder had told him that he was born in Lincolnshire; if he was old enough to be the teacher of John Ive back in the 1480s, he must have been born there before his mother (and father?) moved to Tenterden.[56] Robert Bright of Maidstone, aged sixty years, who admitted to holding dissenting beliefs for at least fourteen years, said he was born at 'Berfold'

[51] See below, 10-13 for the depositions. For John Ive see also below, 5 and *Kentish Visitations*, 72.
[52] See below, 11.
[53] See below, 48.
[54] See below, 87, 95, 100, 116 and 120.
[55] See Thomson, *Later Lollards*, 173-8.
[56] See below, 11. For possible relatives of William Carder who were detected as Lollards in the diocese of Lincoln and elsewhere in the early sixteenth century, see Hudson, *Premature Reformation*, 461-2.

(= Bergholt?) near Ipswich in Suffolk but had left there more than twenty years ago.[57] A link with the Midlands is indicated by a woman who was not involved directly in the present trials, Joan Washingby (or Ward) of Coventry. A prominent Lollard of that city, she had lived for a time in Maidstone, where in 1495 she was forced to abjure her beliefs.[58] There is a need for further research to reveal other links.

The depositions, especially, emphasise the personal side of Lollardy – the 'human touch' to use the words of Richard Davies in his perceptive article, 'for Lollardy was about personal contact and interdependence and drew therefrom its existence and life.'[59] The impression is of a rather democratic and pluralist group of dissenters, though one with a clear sense of identity, at least among its hard-core members. William Carder, for example, appears more as an evangelist than an organiser. The ideological and theological aspects, however, should not be minimised. Certain doctrines had been held with conviction and tenaciously for a long time by a considerable number of the defendants, and were held to the point of death in the case of five of them. These are the minimal conclusions that the proceedings permit: the reality may have been considerably more impressive still, both quantitatively and in terms of sophistication.

vi. Editorial procedure

In the transcription of the manuscript, punctuation and the use of capitals have been modernised and paragraphs have been introduced. The division of words has been modernised (e.g., 'thereabout' not 'there about', 'the same' not 'thesame'). The forms i and j, u and v, have been rationalised and the form ff has been reduced to F or f as appropriate.

Abbreviations have been expanded, except where the contrary is noted by an abbreviation mark ('). Frequently, however, there is an element of conjecture in the expansions, since there is considerable inconsistency in the orthography of the parts of the manuscript in English, with the same word often being spelt differently even within the same sentence.

Headings in capitals and italics, and matter in square brackets, are supplied.

All places in Kent mentioned in the text, as well as Lambeth, are indicated on the Map. The variant spellings of these places that appear in the manuscript are listed underneath the map.

[57] See below, 54 and 95.

[58] C. Cross, 'Great Reasoners in Scripture': The Activities of Women Lollards 1380–1530, in (Ed.) D. Baker, *Medieval Women* (Studies in Church History, Subsidia 1, Oxford 1978), 365–6.

[59] R.G. Davies, 'Lollardy and Locality', *Transactions of the Royal Historical Society*, 6th series, i (1991), 195 and 212.

TABLE 1

The table correlates information about the fifty-three defendants in the proceedings, insofar as it is provided in the manuscript:

Name: in alphabetical order of surnames.

Status in family: d = daughter, h = husband, s = son, w = wife. Home town or village: the place mentioned in their principal entry is given first, followed in brackets by any other places that are mentioned.

Section in this edition: the sections in which they appear as the defendant are given first, followed in brackets by any sections in which they appear as deponents.

Name	Status in family	Home town or village	Age	Occupation	Sections in this edition
Baker, William	h	Cranbrook			10 (6, 7)
Baker, Margaret	w	Cranbrook			15
Bampton, John	h	Boxley (Bearsted, Brasted?, Otham)	33		9 (7)
Bampton, Joyce	w	Bearsted			20
Bampton, Richard		Boxley			20
Baus (Bans?), John		Boxley			22
Benet, John	h	Staplehurst			31
Benet, Rabage	w	Staplehurst			31
Bright, Robert		Maidstone	60	cordwainer	20 (7)
Browne, John		Ashford		cutler	6
Browne, Thomas		Cranbrook			18
Bukherst, John	h	Staplehurst			30
Bukherst, Joan	w	Staplehurst			30
Bukherst, James					31
Bukherst, William				shoemaker	32
Carder, William		Tenterden		weaver (*textor*)	2, 4
Castelyn, Stephen		Tenterden	23	cutler	9, 24 (2, 7)
Chetynden, Agnes		Canterbury			5
Churche, Thomas		Great Chart			14
Colyn, Joan		recently of Tenterden			5
Dodde, John	h	Staplehurst		fletcher	30
Dodde, Joan	w	Staplehurst			30
Felde, Thomas		Boxley			10
Franke, John		Tenterden			19
Franke, Robert		Tenterden			26
Grebill, John senior	h	Benenden (Tenterden)	60	(weaver)[1]	5, 21 (2, 3)
Grebill, Agnes	w	Tenterden (Benenden)	60 *et ultra*		3, 4
Grebill, Christopher	s	Cranbrook (Tenterden)	22	tailor	5 (1, 2, 3)
Grebill, John junior	s	Tenterden	21		5 (3)
Harryson, Robert		Canterbury	60		1, 4
Harwode, Thomas	h	Rolvenden	74		9 (6)

Name	Status in family	Home town or village	Age	Occupation	Sections in this edition
Harwode, Joan	w	Rolvenden			9 (6)
Harwode, Philip	s	Rolvenden	29		9 (6)
Hilles, Robert	h	Tenterden	60		5 (2)
Hilles, Julian	w	Tenterden			25, 29
Hilles, Alice	d	Tenterden	20		15
Ive, Agnes	widow	Canterbury	60		5 (1, 2)
Lorkyn, William		East Farleigh			20
Lowes, Joan		Cranbrook			23
Lynche, John		Tenterden			18
Lynche, Vincent		Halden			16
Mannyng, Thomas		Benenden			5
Olberd, William senior	h	Godmersham			10 (1)
Olberd, Joan	w	Godmersham	63		11
Olberd, William junior	s	Godmersham			10
Pelland, William		Tenterden			28
Piers, Simon		Waldershare			8
Raynold (Reignold), Agnes		Cranbrook		servant	13
Reignold (Reynold), Robert		Cranbrook (Benenden)		10 (7)	
Riche, Joan		Wittersham			17
Riche (Ryche), William		Benenden	40	glover	5 (1, 2, 3, 7)
Walker, Edward		Maidstone		cutler	7
White, Elizabeth		Canterbury			12

[1] The reference to his loom (see below, 11) suggests he was a weaver.

TABLE 2

Folios in the register	Sections in this edition
159r–161v	5
161v–167r	9–20
167r	22
167r–167*v	30–32
167*v–168v	23–25
168v	21
168v–169r	26–27
169r–171v	2–3
171v–172v	1
172v–173r	4
173r–175v	6–8
175v	28–29

TABLE 3

The figures indicate the number of abjurations in which a particular topic appears. The abjurations of forty-six persons survive (counting those that were made in the names of two or more persons – for example, that made in the names of Thomas, Joan and Philip Harwode, below, 61–2 – as two or more abjurations).

The sacraments

38 Eucharist
8 Baptism
7 Confirmation
15 Penance/Confession
7 Priesthood
7 Marriage
6 Last anointing

Others

35 Pilgrimages
35 Images
11 Prayers to saints
9 Blessed bread and holy water
1 'That almighty God our lorde Jhesu Crist, very God eternal withoute begynnyng and very man incarnate, taking flesshe and bloode of the moost pure and glorious virgyn our lady seynt Mary, was God and man incarnate at the begynnyng of the worlde and before he was conceyved and borne of his said blissed moder and virgyn Mary' (below, 59).
1 'That Christ was not incarnatt nor borne of our lady the virgin Mary, nor deed suffer passion for the redempcion of mannys soule, nor dide aryse from deth to lyve the third day aftir his passion' (below, 117).

TABLE 4

The figures indicate the number of persons (total = forty-five, see above, xv) upon whom a particular penance was imposed.

33 Carrying a faggot on a public occasion.
31 Confinement to one's parish or locality.
25 Informing the archbishop of persons suspected of heresy and of books belonging to them.
17 Wearing a badge with a faggot on it.
13 Surrendering heretical books.
12 Attending divine service in one's parish church on Sundays and feast-days.
10 Recitation of the Lord's prayer, Hail Mary and creed.
9 Fasting and/or abstinence.
7 Imprisonment.
7 Confession to a priest.
7 Reception of the eucharist.
7 Watching the execution of William Carder.
6 Restrictions in dress.
3 Offering a candle.
1 Treating his wife well.

Map

Italics indicate the home town or village of one or more defendants, the numbers indicate how many of them (total = fifty-three) came from the place (in a few cases the figure involves some conjecture).

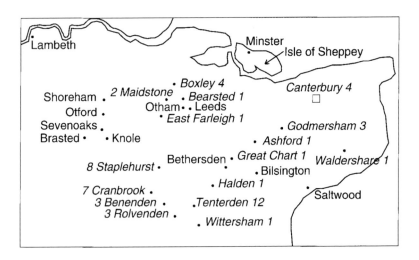

Place	Variant spellings	Place	Variant spellings
Ashford	Assheford	Knole	Knoll
Bearsted	Barsted, Bergstede, Bersted	Lambeth	Lamehith
Benenden	Benynden	Leeds	Leds, Ledys
Bethersden	Batiysden	Maidstone	Maidston
Bilsington		Minster	
Boxley		Otford	
Brasted		Otham	Othan
Canterbury	Cantuar', Cantuariensis,	Rolvenden	Rollynden, Rowenden
	Caunterbury	Saltwood	Saltewode
Chart, see		Sevenoaks	Sevenoke
Great Chart	Crainebroke, Crainbroke	Sheppey	Shepeay, Shepeya
Cranbrook	East Farley	Shoreham	
East Farleigh	Godmarsham	Staplehurst	
Godmersham	Charte, Charte Magna,	Tenterden	Tenderden
Great Chart	Greate Charte, Grete Charte	Waldershare	
		Wittersham	Wittisham
Halden			

KENT HERESY PROCEEDINGS 1511–1512

1. PROCEEDINGS AGAINST ROBERT HARRYSON OF CANTERBURY, 28 APRIL TO 2 MAY, 1511 [fos. 171V–172V]

His appearance in court. Vicesimo octavo die mensis Aprilis anno Domini millesimo quingentesimo undecimo in capella reverendissimi in Christo patris et domini, domini Willelmi[1] permissione divina Cantuariensis archiepiscopi, totius Anglie primatis et apostolice sedis legati, infra manerium suum de Knoll decanatus de Shoreham ecclesie Christi Cantuariensis iurisdictionis immediate, presentibus tunc ibidem venerabilibus viris magistris Cuthberto Tunstall,[2] utriusque iuris doctore, prefati reverendissimi patris cancellario, Thoma Wellis,[3] Gabrieli Silvester,[4] Clemente Browne,[5] sacre theologie professoribus, et pluribus aliis, et in presencia magistrorum Thome Laurence,[6] Willelmi Potkyn et David Cooper, notariorum publicorum, coram eodem reverendissimo patre tunc ibidem pro tribunali iudicialiter sedente, comparuit personaliter Robertus Harryson, nuper de parochia de Halden et nunc de hospitali domus sancti Johannis[7] in parochia beate Marie de Northgate Cantuariensis diocesis, lx annorum etatis. Quem idem reverendissimus pater, ad sancta Dei evangelia per eum tunc ibidem corporaliter tacta, iurare fecit de fideliter respondendo articulis contra eum in negocio heretice pravitatis ex officio eiusdem reverendissimi patris ministratis. Quorum articulorum tenores sequuntur videlicet.

Charges against him. In[a] Dei nomine, Amen. Nos, Willelmus permissione divina Cantuariensis archiepiscopus, totius Anglie primas et

---

[1] William Warham, Archbishop of Canterbury 1503–32.

[2] Appointed as chancellor of Archbishop Warham *c.* 1508 (*BRUO*, iii, 1914), Bishop of London 1522–30, Bishop of Durham 1530–59.

[3] See *BRUO*, iii, 2008–9, Thomas Welles.

[4] See *BRUC*, 573 and 684, Gabriel Sylvester.

[5] See *BRUO*, i, 283–4, Clement Browne.

[6] See *BRUO*, ii, 1108, Thomas Laurens.

[7] Hospital of St. John Baptist in the parish of St. Mary Northgate, in the suburbs of the city of Canterbury.

---

[a] Robertus Harryson *in margin.*

1

apostolice sedis legatus, tibi, Roberto Harryson de Northgate nostre Cantuariensis diocesis ac nostre iurisdictioni notorie subdito et subiecto, ad meram anime tue correctionem necnon ad omne iuris effectum qui exinde sequi poterit aut debebit, obiicimus et articulamur coniunctim et divisim omnes et singulos articulos infrascriptos ac quamlibet partem et particulam [fo. 172r] eorumdem: mandantes et precipientes quatinus eisdem omnibus et singulis singulariterque in eisdem contentis plenam, meram et nudam respondeas veritatem sub pena iuris.

In[b] primis tibi obiicimus et articulamur quod tu fuisti et es nostre Cantuariensis diocesis et nostre iurisdictioni notorie subditus et subiectus.

Item[c] quod tu per plures annos elapsos omnes et singulos hereses, errores et damnatas opiniones subsequentes seu saltem eorum aliquos credidisti, docuisti, tenuisti, affirmasti et predicasti, videlicet.

Quod in sacramento altaris sive eucharistie non est verum corpus Christi.

Item[d] quod sacramenta baptismi et confirmationis non sunt necessaria ad salutem anime.

Item[e] quod vocalis, auricularis sive verbalis confessio peccatorum non est facienda sacerdoti.

Item[f] quod nulla potestas fuit aut est sacerdotibus a Deo collata magis quam laicis in sacramentis ecclesie ministrandis, missis celebrandis aut aliis divinis officiis exequendis.

Item[g] quod matrimonii solemnisatio non est necessaria ad anime salutem nec a iure divino instituta.

Item[h] quod sacramentum extreme unctionis non est utile aut necessarium ad anime salutem.

Item[i] quod ymagines sancte crucis et crucifixi ac beate Marie virginis et aliorum sanctorum nullo modo sunt venerande, sed quod venerantes huiusmodi ymagines committunt idolatriam.

Item[j] quod peregrinationes[k] ad loca sancta et devota, ubi solet populus christianus sanctos et reliquias sanctorum venerari, non sunt necessarie sive meritorie ad salutem anime sed damnabiles, detestando huiusmodi peregrinationes et peregrinantes ad huiusmodi loca reprehendendo, dicendo huiusmodi peregrinantes sic peregrinando committere idolatriam.

Item[l] quod oraciones non sunt effundende ad sanctos sed ad solum Deum, qui solus audit orantes.

Item[m] quod panis benedictus et aqua benedicta non sunt maioris virtutis aut efficacie post benedictionem factam a sacerdote quam ante benedictionem.

---

[b] i in margin.   [c] ii in margin.   [d] iii in margin.   [e] iiii in margin.   [f] v in margin.
[g] vi in margin.   [h] vii in margin.   [i] viii in margin.   [j] ix in margin.
[k] MS. peregrinantes.   [l] x in margin.   [m] xi in margin.

2

Item[n] quod tu omnes et singulos hereses, errores et damnatas opiniones supradictos seu eorum aliquos credis, doces, tenes, affirmas et predicas etiam in presenti.

Item[o] quod tu omnia et singula premissa timore probationum solum et ad evadendam penam es confessus. Et si detecta per alios non fuissent nec timeres te posse convinci per testes, casu quo illa negares premissa numquam sponte confessus fuisses. Nec ea nunc sponte sed timore probationum confiteris.

Item[p] quod tu cum aliis personis de heresibus, erroribus et damnatis opinionibus secum communicantibus sepius et iteratis vicibus communicasti: et ut quod habuisti et habes libros concernentes dictos errores.

His reply to the charges. Deinde idem Robertus Harryson, examinatus super eisdem articulis tunc et ibidem per prefatum reverendissimum patrem, respondet prout sequitur videlicet.

Ad primum articulum respondet et fatetur contenta in eodem esse vera.

Ad secundum et tercium articulos respondet negative.

Ad quartum articulum respondet negative, quia nescit aliter quomodo possit salvari, ut dicit.

Ad quintum, sextum, vii^{mum}, viii^{vum}, ix^{num} et x^{mum} articulos respondet negative.

Ad xi^{mum} articulum respondet negative, et quod credit quod bene prosunt aqua benedicta et panis benedictus et numquam aliter credidit.

Xii^{us} et xiii^{us} articuli pendent ex negatis.

The witnesses. Deinde xxix^{o} die mensis Aprilis anno Domini predicto in aula manerii de Knoll supradicti, prefatus reverendissimus pater in presencia dicti Roberti Harryson produci fecit contra eundem, ad ipsum convincendum in negocio predicto, Willelmum Olberd de Godmersham, Cristoferum Grebill, Agnetem Ive et Laurencium Chetynden de . . .[q]. Quos idem reverendissimus pater iurare fecit ad sancta Dei evangelia per eos et eorum quemlibet corporaliter tacta – amore, timore, odio et favore posthabitis – de dicendo veram et integram veritatem quam noverint de opinionibus dicti Roberti contra fidem catholicam et sacramenta ecclesie. Presentibus tunc ibidem magistris Cuthberto Tunstall, utriusque iuris doctore, Thoma Welles, Gabrieli Silvester et Clemente Browne, sacre theologie professoribus, ac notariis supradictis, cum multis aliis.

Presentation of their depositions. Insuper ultimo die mensis Aprilis anno Domini predicto in capella manerii de Knoll supradicti, coram

---

[n] xii *in margin.*   [o] xiii *in margin.*   [p] xiiii *in margin.*   [q] *Blank space in MS.*

antedicto reverendissimo in Christo patre pro tribunali iudicialiter
sedente, comparuit personaliter dictus Robertus Harryson. In cuius
presentia idem reverendissimus pater tunc ibidem publicavit dicta et
depositiones testium productorum contra eundem[r] et per eundem
reverendissimum patrem examinatorum. Et huiusmodi testium dicta in
presencia eiusdem Roberti publice perlegi fecit. Et assignavit eidem
Roberto ad dicendum contra eosdem testes, et ad alias proponendum
que faciant pro sua defensione legitima, diem Veneris proximum in
capella predicta, ulteriusque ad procedi videndum ad ulteriora in
huiusmodi negocio contra eundem Robertum. Presentibus tunc ibidem
reverendissimo patre Johanne Sironense episcopo,[8] venerabilibusque
viris magistris Cuthberto Tunstall, utriusque iuris doctore, Roberto
Wodwarde,[9] decretorum doctore, Gabrieli Silvestre, sacre theologie
professore, Roberto Ascom,[10] artium magistro, Johanne Peers,[11] in
decretis bacallario, ac pluribus aliis una cum notariis prerecitatis.
Quorum testium dicta et depositiones sequuntur videlicet.

Deposition of Christopher Grebill. Cristofer Grebill of Crainebroke,
taylor, of the diocise of Caunterbury of the age of xxii[ti] yeres, sworn
and examynd how Robert Harryson of seynt Johns of Caunterbury hath
belyved in the vii sacraments and other techings of holy church, he
saith and deposith upon his othe that, upon the even of the assumption
of our Lady last past, this deponent and the saide Robert Harryson
goyng by the waye betwen the Grete Charte and Batiysden, whan and
where he hard the said Robert Harryson say that pilgremage goyng was
not profitable to a mannys soule but it was but lost labor. And in
lykewise the said Robert said of indulgences and pardons to be of noon
effecte nor profitt, and that mony or candels offered to images in the
churche was nor profitable for mannys soule.

Examyned who was then there present, he saith that noon other
persone or persones that herd the said communicacion but oonly they
twoo. Examyned further whether he had ever any communicacion with
the saide Harryson ayenst any of the vii sacraments, he saith and
aunswereth that there was never suche communicacion betwix them

---

[8] John Thornden, a Benedictine monk who as *episcopus Sironensis/Cironensis* (Cyrene
in Palestine) acted as suffragan to the archbishop of Canterbury between 1508 and 1514
(Eds. E.B. Fryde and others, *Handbook of British Chronology*, 3rd edn., London, 1986,
286).
[9] See *BRUO*, iii, 2085, Robert Woodward.
[10] See *BRUO*, i, 55, Robert Ashcombe.
[11] See *BRUO*, iii, 1482, John Piers.

[r] productorum *repeated.*

ayenst any of the vii sacraments. Item as touching pilgremages and offerings to images of seynts, this deponent saith that he and the said Haryson oonly by themself had diverse tymes communicacions therof as is afore rehersed.

Deposition of William Ryche. William Ryche of Benynden of the diocise of Caunterbury, glover, of the age of xl yeres, sworn and examyned how Robert Haryson of Caunterbury hath belyved and comyned of the sacrament of the aulter, he saith and deposith that ii yeres passed at Tenterden upon seynt Marks day, at a feyre kept there, he had communicacion with the said Haryson and herd hym say that the blissed sacrament of the aulter was not the verey body of Crist but oonly materyall brede.

Examyned who was moo present at that tyme of the said communicacion, he saith that there was noon other body hard the said communicacion but oonly they ii to his knowledge. And at divers and sondry tymes sith that tyme this deponent saith that they ii hath comyned ayenst the blissed sacrament of the aulter as well at Caunterbury as at Tenterden. Examyned who was present at the said communicacion at Caunterbury, this deponent saith that in the even or the day of the translacion of [fo. 172v] saynt Thomas, was xii moneth, he cam to the house of John Ive in Caunterbury in the company of the said Harryson at his desire, where and when they founde the said John Ive and William Olberd the elder. And at the same tyme the said deponent with the said Robert Haryson, John Ive and William Olberd and every oon of them had communicacion and herd the said Robert and every of theym say and speke ayenst the blissed sacrament of the aulter, saying and affirmyng that it was not the verey body of Crist but oonly brede.

Deposition of William Olberd senior. William Olberd the elder of Godmersham of the diocese of Caunterbury of the age of lxiiii yeres, sworn and examyned how Robert Harryson of Canterbury hath belived and commyned of the blissed sacrament of the aulter, he aunswereth and saith upon his othe that upon the fest of the translacion of seynt Thomas yat last was, was xii moneth, in the house of John Ive in Caunterbury decessid, the same John Ive, Robert Haryson and William Riche and this deponent then and there had communicacion togider ayenst the sacrament of the aulter. And this deponent saith that then and there he herd the said John Ive, Robert Haryson and William Riche and every of theym say and afferme that in the sacrament of the aulter was not the verey flesshe and body of Criste but oonly materiall bred. And soo all they fowre persones and every of theym then and there fully concludid and belyved.

5

Deposition of Agnes Ive. Agnes Ive, wydow, of the parisshe of seynt
George in Caunterbury of the age of lx yeres and more, sworn and
examyned how Robert Haryson of Caunterbury hath beleved and
commyned of the sacrament off the aulter and in other of the vii
sacraments and techings of the holy churche, she saith and deposith that
at this half, the fest of all Seynts last passed, oon Elizabeth White of
Caunterbury desyred this deponent to goo with hir to Robert Harysons
house beside saynt Johns hospital yn Caunterbury, and soo she dide.
And at theyr comyng togider thider to the said Robert Haryson, he
beyng there present, she hard hym spek and comyn of pilgremages as
she now remembreth and thynketh. And as this deponent thynketh and
supposith, that the said Harryson wolde have talked and had further
communicacion of other things touching the vii sacraments but that he
was lettid by the comyng yn into the said house of a certeyn broder of
the hospital of seynt[s] Johns aforsaid. And otherwise she cannot depose
of the said Haryson, but by the reporte and saying of hir husband and of
the said Elizabeth White divers and sondry tymes, whom she hath herd
divers tymes reporte that the said Haryson was of their secte, beleve and
opynion ayenst the sacraments of the churche.

His reply, and declaration of the sentence. Item, secundo die mensis
Maii anno Domini et loco predictis, coram reverendissimo patre pro
tribunali tunc ibidem iudicialiter sedente, comparuit personaliter dictus
Robertus Harryson, habens hos diem et locum et prefixione iudiciali ad
dicendum contra testes et ad proponendum quecumque noverit pro sua
defensione legitima quare pro heretico convicto pronunciari et declarari
non debeat. Qui quidem Robertus, tunc ibidem ut prefertur personaliter
constitutus, nichil allegavit aut proposuit pro se in ea parte sed se
ecclesie submisit. Unde dictus reverendissimus pater sententiam contra
eundem in scriptis tunc ibidem tulit diffinitivam, ipsum pro heretico
impenitente et incorrigibili pronunciando et manui seculari relin-
quendo. Cuius sentencie tenor sequitur et est talis.

Sentence. In[t] Dei nomine, Amen. Nos, Willelmus permissione divina
Cantuariensis archiepiscopus, totius Anglie primas et apostolice sedis
legatus, in quodam negocio heretice pravitatis contra te, Robertum
Haryson civitatis nostre Cantuariensis laicum ac nostre iurisdictioni
notorie subditum et subiectum, coram nobis in iudicio personaliter
comparentem, nobis super heretica pravitate huiusmodi detectum et
delatum ac per nostram diocesim Cantuariensem antedictam notorie et
publice in ea parte apud bonos et graves diffamatum, ex officio nostro

[s] saynt *follows* seynt.   [t] Sententia contra Haryson *in margin.*

mero, rite et canonice procedentes – auditis et intellectis, visis, cognitis rimatisque ac matura deliberatione discussis et ponderatis dicti negocii meritis, servatisque in omnibus et per omnia in eodem negocio de iure servandis ac quomodolibet requisitis – pro tribunali sedentes, Christi nomine invocato, et solum Deum pre oculis habentes.

Quia per acta, actitata, deducta, probata et exhibita coram nobis in eodem negocio invenimus te per probationes legitimas coram nobis in hac parte iudicialiter factas nonnullos et varios errores, hereses et damnatas opiniones iuri divino et ecclesiastico obviantes, contrarios et repugnantes contra fidem orthodoxam per universalem, catholicam et apostolicam ecclesiam determinatam et observatam tenuisse, credidissse, affirmasse, predicasse et dogmatisasse et presertim contra sacramenta altaris seu eucharistie et alia sacramenta et sancte matris ecclesie dogmata. Et quatinus nos, Christi vestigiis inherendo, qui non vult mortem peccatoris sed magis ut convertatur et vivat, sepe numero conati fuimus te corrigere ac viis et modis licitis et canonicis, quibus potuimus aut scivimus, ad fidem orthodoxam per universalem catholicam et apostolicam ecclesiam determinatam et observatam ac ad unitatem eiusdem sancte matris ecclesie reducere. Tamen invenimus te adeo dure cervicis quod tuos errores et hereses huiusmodi nolueris sponte et incontinenti confiteri, nec ad fidem catholicam et unitatem sancte matris ecclesie antedictas debite reverti et redire. Sed tanquam iniquitatis filius et tenebrarum filius in tantum indurasti cor tuum ut non velis intelligere vocem tui pastoris tibi parterno compacientis affectu. Nec velis piis et paternis monicionibus allici nec salubribus reduci blandiciis.

Nos vero, nolentes quod tu qui nequam es fias nequior, et gregem dominicum in futurum tua heretice pravitatis labe de quo plurimum timemus inficias, idcirco, de consilio iurisperitorum nobis in hac parte assistentium cum quibus communicavimus in hac parte, te, Robertum predictum, demeritis atque culpis per tuam damnabilem petinaciam aggravatis, de et super huiusmodi detestabili heretice pravitatis reatu convictum et ad ecclesie unitatem penitencialiter redire nolentem, hereticum hereticisque credentem ac eorum fautorem et receptatorem pretextu premissorum fuisse et esse, cum dolore et amaritudine cordis iudicamus et declaramus sentencialiter et diffinitive in his scriptis: relinquentes te ex nunc tanquam hereticum iudicio sive curie seculari. Teque Robertum predictum, ut prefertur, hereticum nichilominus in maioris excommunicationis sentenciam occasione premissorum incidisse et incurrisse, necnon excommunicatum fuisse et esse pronunciamus, decernimus et declaramus etiam in his scriptis.

Presentibus tunc ibidem reverendo patre domino Johanne, Sironense episcopo, ac venerabilibus viris magistris Cuthberto Tunstall, utriusque iuris doctore, Thoma Welles, Gabrieli Silvester et Clemente Browne, sacre theologie professoribus, una cum notariis supradictis ac multis aliis.

2. PROCEEDINGS AGAINST WILLIAM CARDER OF TENTERDEN, 29 APRIL TO 2 MAY, 1511 [fos. 169R–170R]

His appearance in court. Vicesimo nono die mensis Aprilis anno Domini millesimo quingentesimo undecimo in aula manerii reverendissimi patris et domini, domini Willelmi permissione divina Cantuariensis archiepiscopi, totius Anglie primatis et apostolice sedis legati, de Knoll decanatus de Shoreham iurisdictionis immediate, coram eodem reverendissimo patre tunc ibidem pro tribunali iudicialiter sedente, presentibus tunc ibidem venerabilibus viris magistris Cuthberto Tunstall, utriusque iuris doctore, eiusdem reverendissimi patris cancellario, Gabrieli Silvester, Thoma Wellys et Clemente Browne, sacre theologie professoribus, et aliis, in presencia etiam magistrorum Thome Laurence, Willelmi Potkyn et David Cooper, notariorum publicorum, comparuit personaliter Willelmus Carder[a] de Tenterden, textor, super crimine heretice pravitatis detectus. Quem idem reverendissimus pater tunc ibidem, ad sancta Dei evangelia per eum corporaliter tacta, iurari fecit de fideliter respondendo articulis infrascriptis contra eum ex officio dicti reverendissimi patris obiectis. Quorum articulorum tenores sequuntur videlicet.

Charges against him. In Dei nomine, Amen. Nos, Willelmus permissione divina Cantuariensis archiepiscopus, totius Anglie primas et apostolice sedis legatus, tibi, Willelmo Carder de Tenterden nostre Cantuariensis diocesis ac nostre iurisdictioni notorie subdito et subiecto, ad meram anime tue correctionem necnon ad omne iuris effectum qui exinde sequi poterit aut debebit, obiicimus et articulamur coniunctim et divisim omnes et singulos articulos infrascriptos ac quamlibet partem et particulam eorundem: mandantes et precipientes quatinus eisdem omnibus et singulis singulariterque in eisdem contentis plenam, meram et nudam respondeas veritatem sub pena iuris.

In[b] primis tibi obiicimus et articulamur quod tu fuisti et es nostre Cantuariensis diocesis ac nostre iurisdictioni notorie subditus et subiectus.

Item[c] quod tu plures annos elapsos omnes et singulos hereses, errores et damnatas opiniones subsequentes seu saltem eorum aliquos credidisti, docuisti, tenuisti, affirmasti et predicasti, videlicet.

Quod in sacramento altaris sive eucharistie non est verum corpus Christi sed panis materialis.

Item[d] quod sacramenta baptismi et confirmationis non sunt necessaria ad salutem anime.

---

[a] Willelmus Carder *also in margin.*   [b] i *in margin.*   [c] ii *in margin.*   [d] iii *in margin.*

Item^e quod vocalis, auricularis sive verbalis confessio peccatorum non est facienda sacerdoti.

Item^f quod nulla potestas fuit aut est sacerdotibus a Deo collata magis quam laicis in sacramentis ecclesie ministrandis, missis celebrandis aut aliis divinis officiis exequendis.

Item^g quod matrimonii solemnisatio non est necessaria ad anime salutem nec a iure divino instituta.

Item^h quod sacramentum ultime unctionis non est utile aut necessarium ad anime salutem.

Itemⁱ quod imagines sancte crucis et crucifixe ac beate Marie virginis et aliorum sanctorum nullo modo sunt venerande, sed quod venerantes huiusmodi imagines committunt idolatriam.

Item^j quod peregrinationes ad loca sancta et devota, ubi solet populus christianus sanctos et reliquias sanctorum venerari, non sunt necessarie sive meritorie ad salutem anime sed damnabiles, detestando huiusmodi peregrinationes et peregrinantes ad huiusmodi loca reprehendo, dicendo huiusmodi peregrinantes sic peregrinando committere ydolatriam.

Item^k quod orationes non sunt effundende ad sanctos sed ad solum Deum, qui solus audit orantes.

Item^l quod panis benedictus et aqua benedicta non sunt maioris virtutis et efficatie post benediccionem factam a sacerdote quam ante benedictionem.

Item^m quod tu omnes et singulos hereses, errores et damnatas opiniones supradictos seu eorum aliquos credis, doces, tenes, affirmas et predicas etiam in presenti.

Itemⁿ quod tu omnia et singula premissa timore probationum solum et ad evadendam penam es confessus. Et si detecta per alios non fuissent nec timeres te posse convinci per testes, casu quo illa negares premissa nunquam sponte confessus fuisses. Nec ea nunc sponte sed timore probationum confiteris.

Item^o quod tu cum aliis personis de prefatis heresibus, erroribus et damnatis opinionibus secum communicantibus sepius et iteratis vicibus communicasti: et ut quod habuisti et habes libros concernentes dictos errores.

His reply to the charges. Deinde idem Willelmus Carder, examinatus tunc ibidem in presencia supradicta super interrogatoriis antedictis, respondit prout sequitur videlicet.

Ad primum articulum respondet et fatetur contenta in eodem esse vera.

---

^e iiii *in margin.*   ^f v *in margin.*   ^g vi *in margin.*   ^h vii *in margin.*   ⁱ viii *in margin.*
^j ix *in margin.*   ^k x *in margin.*   ^l xi *in margin.*   ^m xii *in margin.*   ⁿ xiii *in margin.*
^o xiiii *in margin.*

9

Ad secundum articulum respondet negative sic in vulgari videlicet. That he beleveth and hath ever beleved that the sacrament of the aulter is very Crists [fo. 169v] body, flesshe and bloode; and that he hath never commyned with no man nor no man with hym to the contrary. Ad tercium articulum dicit sic videlicet. That Robert Reignold of Tenterden, the Friday of the first weke in Lent last past, came and dyned at this deponents house and there redde in a booke and sermon of seynt Austyn spekyng ageynst the sacrament of baptisme. And aftir that he had redde it he askid of this deponent: 'How say ye nowe of the opinion of heretiks, what avayleth to cristen a childe in colde water?' And this deponent aunswered agayn: 'Ye be full of questyons, beleve ye as ye will: I woll beleve as a cristen man shuld do.' Ad cetera contenta in hoc articulo respondet negative.

Ad quartum, quintum, sextum et septimum respondet negative.

Ad viii^{vum} articulum respondet negative, dicendo sic. That he trusteth to have made for goyng in pilgremages and offerings to images of seynts.

Ad ix^{num} respondet negative.

Ad x^{mum} sic respondet videlicet. That it is ynough to pray to God almighty and alone and therfore it nedith not to pray to seynts for any mediacion.

Ad xi^{mum} respondet negative.

Xii^{mus} et xiii^{mus} articuli pendent ex negatis.

Ad xiii^{mum} articulum respondet negative.

The witnesses. Deinde ultima die mensis Aprilis anno Domini, loco et presencia personarum superius specificatarum, coram prefato reverendissimo patre ut supra pro tribunali sedente, comparuit personaliter dictus Willelmus Carder. Contra quem idem reverendissimus pater, ad convincendum eundem, produci fecit in eiusdem Willelmi presencia Cristoferum Grebill de Tenterden, Willelmum Riche de Benynden, Agnetem Ive civitatis Cantuariensis, Johannem Grebill senior, Robertum Hilles de Tenterden et Stephanum Castelyn de Tenterden, in testes. Quos idem reverendissimus pater, ad sancta Dei evangelia per eos et eorum quemlibet tunc ibidem corporaliter tacta, iurari fecit de dicendo omnem et omnimodam veritatem – amore, timore et favore semotis – quam noverint de opinionibus prefati Willelmi Carder contra sacramenta ecclesie et fidem catholicam. Quorum quidem testium dicta et depositiones sequuntur videlicet.

Deposition of Robert Hilles. Robert Hilles of the parisshe of Tenterden of the diocise of Caunterbury of the age of lx yeres, sworn and examyned of the belyve of William Carder of Tenterden, saith that the same William hath and yet doeth, as he thynketh, belyve that the sacrament of the aulter ys not Crists very body but verey brede; that the sacrament of penance and confession was nothing worth; and the auctoritie and power of preests upon sacraments and other things by them mynistred was no more worth than if they had be doon by a layman, and that they had no more power than another; item that it was not nede to pray to any seynt but oonly to God.

Examyned how he knoweth that the said Cardar soo hath belyved, he saith that in the house of this deponent ii tymes aboute ii yeres past, and bifore that atte hale houses and in the said Cardirs house and churche and other places, the saide William Cardar taught this deponent the said errors, saying that he dide soo belive and conseilled this deponent to doo in lykewise. Examyned who were present, he saith that noon other persone but they ii at noe season sayyng that when they went about those maters they wold have noon of their counseill.

Deposition of John Grebill senior. John Grebill the elder of Benynden of the diocise of Caunterbury, lx yeres of age, sworn and examyned upon the beleve of the said William Carder in the sacraments of the church and the articles of the faith, saith that the said William Carder hath belived ayenst the sacrament of the aulter that it is not Crists body but verey oonly brede; that confession was nothing worth; and that all the vii sacraments were nought; and ther shuld no prayers nor worship be made to any seynts in heven but oonly God.

Examyned how he knoweth this, he aunswerith and saith that the said William Cardar, about xx^{ti} yeres past in the house of this deponent at Tenderden werkyng in his lome, the said William Cardar[p] began first to rede in a booke of ii evangelists and teche this deponent of the said his belyves. And from aftirward this deponent removyng to Benynden, thens divers many tymes and last in wynter last passid at Benynden and divers other places whan they mought mete togider secretly without suspicion, than the said William Carder taught this deponent to beleve as ys abovesaid, saying that he belevid soo. And in comenyng togider they bothe agreed and bileved. He saith ferther that he thynketh that the said was borne in Lincolnshyre and that the said Carder shewed to this deponent that his fader and moder were of the same secte. And he saith that the moder of the said Cardar fled from Tenterden about xl yeres past for fere of the saide heresies, but whether he knoweth not.

Examyned who were present at any of their communicacions, he saith noon. Except that he supposith that oon tyme Cristofer Grebill was present whan Carder was with hym att wynter last past. But noon other, for they wold never make any man of counseill when they were about suche matiers; saving that betwixt Cristmas and Shroftyde last

[p] the said William Cardar *repeated sic.*

11

past, the saide Carder beyng in this deponents house when this deponent went owte of his house, he left the said Carder commenyng with this deponents wife.

Deposition of Stephen Castellen. Stephen Castellen of Tenterden of the age of xxiii^{ti} yeres, cutler, sworn and examyned, saith that William Carder of Tenterden taught hym first to belive ayenst the sacrament of the aulter, that it was not Goddes body, flesshe and bloode, but oonly brede, in Maydeston aboute a iii yeres agoo.

Deposition of Agnes Ive. Agnes Ive of the parisshe of seynt George of Caunterbury, lx yeres of age, late wif of John Ive, sworn and examyned how William Carder of Tenterden beleveth of the sacraments and doctryne of holy churche, she saith that she thynketh that the said William Carder belived ayenst the sacrament of the aulter, that it was but very brede and not Crists body, and also ayenst all the sacraments.

Examyned how she supposith or knoweth that, she saith by hir husbond, John Ive, which alwayes said that this William Carder was his techer and reder. She herd it also of hir brother, Robert Hilles, and John Grebill the elder, which said of the same Carder that he beleved and taught theym that the sacrament of the aulter was not Crists verey body but oonly brede, and that all the other sacraments were of noon effect nor profitable for mannys soule. And otherwise she cannot depose as she saithe.

Deposition of William Ryche. William Ryche of Benynden, glover, of the age of xl yeres, sworn and examyned of the belyve of William Carder of Tenterden, he saith that the said Carder beleved, hold and taught that the sacrament of the aulter ys but verey brede and not Crists body, and also ayenst all the sacraments and teching of the churche.

Examyned how he knowith that, he saith that he hath commyned with the said Carder divers tymes thies viii yeres past, and now last at Benynden in this deponents house yn the wynter tyme last passed, and often tymes bifore at Tenterden and other places, when and where they myght be secretly togider; they then commenyng and holding the said opinions ayenst the sacrament of the aulter, that it was but verey brede and not Crists body, and ayenst all the other sacraments and teching of holy churche, that [fo. 170r] they be nothing profitable for mannys soule.

Examyned who were present at their suche communicacions and holding of opinions, he saith no persone at no tyme, for they wold never make anybody privey nor of conseill when^q they went aboute suche maters.

q *MS.* went.

Deposition of Christopher Grebill. Cristofer Grebill of Tenterden of the diocise of Caunterbury, taylor, sworn and examyned of the belive of William Carder of Tenterden, how he hath belived of the sacraments and teching of holy church, he saith that the same William Carder ys of the said mysbileve ayenst the sacrament of the aulter, that it is but brede and not Crists body, and in likewise he helde and beleved ayenst all other sacraments and teching of the holy churche, that they be not profitable for mannys soule nor anything worth.

Examyned how he knoweth thus, he saith that he was present in wynter last past whan the said Carder came to the house of this deponents faders[r] in Benynden and there taught and commyned with his said fader and with this deponent yn the said hous ayenst the sacrament of the aulter, that it was not Crists body but oonly brede, and also ayenst all other sacraments and doctrynes of the holy churche, saying that they were nothing avaylable for mannys soule but all unprofitable. He saith that according to his teching he dide bileve. And the said William Carder, John Grebill his fader, and he hymself togider aggreed, hild and affermed all the same opinions and errors. Saying Cristofer Grebill also that the saide Carder hath been the myschief and destruccion of many men, by bringyng theym into the said mysbileves ayenst the sacrament of the aulter, that it is but oonly bede, and that all other sacraments be not profitable for mannys soule, in bryngyng of . . .[s] Reignold therto, and also William Baker. Which William shewed to this deponent that he was brought to the said error ayenst the sacrament of the aulter, that it was but brede, and the other sacraments not profitable for mannys soule, by the said Carder; but that it was long er the said Carder cowde bring hym to it so to belive.

Presentation of the depositions. Insuper, die et loco immediate predictis, prefatus reverendissimus pater pro tribunali iudicialiter [sedens], presentibus tunc ibidem reverendo patre domino Johanne Sironense episcopo ac venerabilibus viris magistris Cuthberto Tunstall, utriusque iuris, Roberto Wodwarde, decretorum, Gabrieli Silvester, sacre pagine, doctoribus, Roberto Ascom, artium magistro, Johanne Pieris, in discretis[t] baccallario, et aliis, in presencia etiam notariorum supradictorum, in presencia dicti Willelmi Carder, publicavit et publice perlegi fecit dicta et depositiones testium supradictorum. Et assignavit eidem Willelmo Carder pro termino ad dicendum contra huiusmodi testes, si velit, et ad proponendum omnia que faciunt pro sua defensione legitima in hac parte, diem Veneris proximum ex tunc futurum in aula predicta.

---

[r] faders *sic.*   [s] *Blank space in MS.*   [t] discretis *sic, here and elsewhere.*

13

His reply, and declaration of the sentence. Quo die adveniente,
videlicet secundo Maii anno Domini supradicto, in aula supradicta,
presentibus tunc ibidem reverendo patre domino Johanne Sironense
episcopo ac venerabilibus viris magistris Cuthberto Tunstall predicto,
Thoma Welles, Gabrieli Silvester et Clemente Browne, sacre theologie
professoribus, ac notariis superius specificatis, coram prefato reverendo
patre pro tribunali sedente, comparuit personaliter dictus Willelmus
Carder: habens hos diem et locum pro termino ad dicendum contra
dicta testium predictorum, iterum tunc ibidem in eiusdem Willelmi
presencia recitata et publice perlecta ac per eosdem testes tunc ibidem
coram dicto Willelmo facie ad faciem affirmata. Quibus sic gestis, ipse
Willelmus Carder dixit quod noluit contradicere deposicionibus et
attestationibus huiusmodi. Et dixit insuper quod si male unquam senciit
contra sacramenta ecclesie vel fidem catholicam, penitet eum. Sed dicit
quod non recordatur si unquam male sencisse seu dixisse contra
sacramenta huiusmodi aut fidem catholicam. Interrogatus ulterius si
habet aliquid aliud per eum allegandum quare sentencia contra eum
ferri non debeat, respondet et dicit quod nichil habet aut vult allegare in
ea parte. Quamobrem idem reverendissimus pater sentenciam contra
eundem Willelmum Carder tunc ibidem tulit in scriptis, per quam
ipsum hereticum impenitentem et incorrigibilem declaravit et
pronunciavit. Cuius sentencie tenor sequitur.

Sentence. In[u] Dei nomine, Amen. Nos, Willelmus permissione divina
Cantuariensis archiepiscopus, totius Anglie primas et apostolice sedis
legatus, in quodam negocio heretice pravitatis contra te, Willelmum
Carder de Tenterden nostre Cantuariensis diocesis laicum ac nostre
iurisdictioni notorie subditum et subiectum, coram nobis in iudicio
personaliter comparentem, nobis super heretica pravitate huiusmodi
detectum et delatum ac per nostram diocesim Cantuariensem
antedictam notorie et publice in ea parte apud bonos et graves diffamatum, ex officio nostro mero, rite et canonice procedentes – auditis et
intellectis, visis, cognitis rimatisque ac matura deliberatione discussis
et ponderatis dicti negocii meritis, servatisque in omnibus et per omnia
in eodem negocio de iure servandis ac quomodolibet requisitis – pro
tribunali sedentes, Christi nomine invocato, et solum Deum pre oculis
habentes.

Quia per acta, actitata, deducta, probata et exhibita coram nobis in
eodem negocio invenimus te per probationes legitimas coram nobis in
hac parte iudicialiter factas nonnullos et varios errores, hereses et
dampnatas opiniones iuri divino et ecclesiastico obviantes, contrarios et
repugnantes contra fidem orthodoxam per universalem catholicam et

---

[u] Sentencia contra Carder *in margin.*

14

apostolicam ecclesiam determinatam et observatam tenuisse, credidisse, affirmasse, predicasse et dogmatisasse et presertim contra sacramenta altaris seu eucharistie, penitencie, ordinis et alia sacramenta et sancte matris ecclesie dogmata. Et quia nos, Christi vestigiis inherendo, qui non vult mortem peccatoris sed magis ut convertatur et vivat, sepe numero conati fuimus te corrigere ac viis et modis licitis et canonicis, quibus potuimus aut scivimus, ad fidem orthodoxam per universalem, catholicam et apostolicam ecclesiam determinatam et observatam ac ad unitatem eiusdem sancte matris ecclesie reducere. Tamen invenimus te adeo dure cervicis quod tuos errores et hereses huiusmodi nolueris sponte et incontinenti confiteri, nec ad fidem catholicam et unitatem sancte matris ecclesie antedictas debite reverti et redire. Sed tanquam iniquitatis et tenebrarum filius in tantum indurasti cor tuum ut non velis intelligere vocem tui pastoris tibi paterno compacientis affectu. Nec velis piis et paternis monitionibus allici nec salubribus reduci blandiciis.

Nos vero, nolentes quod tu qui nequam es fias nequior, et gregem dominicum in futurum tua heretice pravitatis labe de quo plurimum timemus inficias, idcirco, de consilio iurisperitorum nobis in hac parte assistentium cum quibus communicavimus in hac parte, te, Willelmum Carder, predictis demeritis atque culpis per tuam damnabilem pertinaciam aggravatis, de et super huiusmodi detestabili heretice pravitatis reatu convictum et ad ecclesie unitatem penitencialiter redire nolentem, hereticum hereticisque credentes ac eorum fautorem et receptatorem pretextu premissorum fuisse et esse, cum dolore et amaritudine cordis indicamus et declaramus sentencialiter et diffinitive in his scriptis: relinquentes te ex tunc tanquam hereticum iudicio sive curie seculari. Teque, Willelmum Carder predictum ut prefertur hereticum, nichilominus in maioris excommunicationis sentenciam occasione premissorum incidisse et incurrisse, necnon excommunicatum fuisse et esse, pronunciamus, decernimus et declaramus etiam in hiis scriptis.

15

3. PROCEEDINGS AGAINST AGNES GREBILL OF TENTERDEN, 29 APRIL TO
2 MAY, 1511 [fos. 170R–171V]

Her appearance in court. Vicesimo nono die mensis Aprilis anno
Domini millesimo quingentesimo undecimo in capella manerii
reverendissimi in Christo patris et domini, domini Willelmi permissione divina Cantuariensis archiepiscopi, totius Anglie primatis et
apostolice sedis legati, de Knoll decanatus de Shoreham ecclesie
Christi Cantuariensis iurisdictionis immediate, coram eodem
reverendissimo patre tunc ibidem pro tribunali [fo. 170v] iudicialiter
sedente, presentibus tunc ibidem venerabilibus[a] viris magistris
Cuthberto Tunstall, utriusque iuris doctore, eiusdem reverendissimi
patris cancellario, Gabrieli Silvester, Thoma Welles et Clemente
Browne, sacre theologie professoribus, et aliis, in presencia etiam
magistrorum Thome Laurence, Willelmi Potkyn et David Cooper,
notariorum publicorum, comparuit personaliter Agnes Grebill,[b] uxor
Johannis Grebill senior, de Tenterden, etatis lx annorum et ultra. Quam
idem reverendissimus pater, ad sancta Dei evangelia per eam
corporaliter tacta, iurari fecit de fideliter respondendo certis articulis
contra eam in negocio heretice pravitatis ex officio dicti reverendissimi
patris ministratis. Quorum articulorum tenor sequitur videlicet.

Charges against her. In Dei nomine, Amen. Nos, Willelmus permissione divina Cantuariensis archiepiscopus, totius Anglie primas et
apostolice sedis legatus, tibi, Agneti Grebill nostre Cantuariensis
diocesis ac nostre iurisdictioni notorie subdite et subiecte, ad meram
anime tue correctionem necnon ad omnem iuris effectum qui exinde
sequi poterit aut debebit, obiicimus et articulamur coniunctim et divisim
omnes et singulos articulos infrascriptos ac quamlibet partem et
particulam eorundem: mandantes et precipientes quatinus eisdem
omnibus et singulis singulariterque in eisdem contentis plenam, meram
et nudam respondeas veritatem sub pena iuris.
  In primis tibi obiicimus et articulamur quod tu fuisti et es nostre
diocesis ac nostre iurisdictioni notorie subdita et subiecta.[c]
  Item[d] quod tu plures annos elapsos omnes et singulos hereses,
errores et damnatas opiniones subsequentes seu saltem eorum aliquos
credidisti, docuisti, tenuisti, affirmasti et predicasti, videlicet.
  Quod in sacramento altaris sive eucharistie non est verum corpus
Christi sed panis materialis.
  Item[e] quod sacramenta baptismi et confirmacionis non sunt
necessaria ad salutem anime.

---

[a] venerabilibus *repeated.*   [b] Agnes Grebill *also in margin.*
[c] *MS.* subditus et subiectus.   [d] ii *in margin.*   [e] iii *in margin.*

Item^f quod vocalis, auricularis sive verbalis confessio peccatorum [non] est facienda sacerdoti.

Item^g quod nulla potestas fuit aut est sacerdotibus a Deo collata magis quam laicis in sacramentis ecclesie ministrandis, missis celebrandis aut aliis divinis officiis exequendis.

Item^h quod matrimonii solemnisatio non est necessaria ad anime salutem nec a iure divino instituta.

Itemⁱ quod sacramentum extreme unctionis non est utile aut necessarium ad anime salutem.

Item^j quod imagines sancte crucis et crucifixi ac beate Marie virginis et aliorum sanctorum nullo modo sunt venerande, sed quod venerantes huiusmodi imagines committunt idolatriam.

Item^k quod peregrinaciones ad loca sancta et devota, ubi solet populus christianus sanctos et reliquias sanctorum venerari, non sunt necessarie sive meritorie ad salutem anime sed damnabiles, detestando huiusmodi peregrinationes et peregrinantes ad hjuiusmodi loca reprehendendo, dicendo huiusmodi peregrinantes sic peregrinando committere idolatriam.

Item^l quod oraciones non sunt effundende ad sanctos sed ad solum Deum, qui solus audit orantes.

Item^m quod panis benedictus et aqua benedicta non sunt maioris virtutis et efficacie post benedictionem factam a sacerdote quam ante benedictionem.

Itemⁿ quod tu omnes et singulos hereses, errores et damnatas opiniones supradictas seu eorum aliquos credis, doces, tenes, affirmas et predicas etiam in presenti.

Item^o quod tu omnia et singula premissa timore probationum solum et ad evadendam penam es confessus. Et si detecta per alios non fuissent nec timeres te posse convinci per testes, casu quo illa negares premissa nunquam sponte confessus fuisses. Nec ea nunc sponte sed timore probationum confiteris.

Item^p quod tu cum aliis personis de prefatis heresibus, erroribus et damnatis opinionibus secum communicantibus sepius et iteratis vicibus communicasti: et ut quod habuisti et habes libros concerntes dictos errores.

Her reply to the charges. Ad primum articulum respondet et fatetur. Ad secundum articulum respondet negative, sic dicendo in vulgari videlicet: that she hath alwayes beleved in the sacrament of the aulter, that it is the body of God. Ad tercium articulum respondet etiam

---

^f iv *in margin.* ^g v *in margin.* ^h vi *in margin.* ⁱ vii *in margin.* ^j viii *in margin.*
^k ix *in margin.* ^l x *in margin.* ^m xi *in margin.* ⁿ xii *in margin.* ^o xiii *in margin.*
^p xiiii *in margin.*

17

negative, dicendo sic: that she hath alwayes beleved, and so doeth beleve, that by baptising the child ys delivered owte of origynall synne. Ad iiii^{tum}, v^{tum}, sextum, septimum, viii^{vum}, ix^{num}, x^{um}, xi^{um}, xii, xiii et xiiii^{um} articulos respondet negative ad singula contenta in eisdem.

The witnesses. Deinde prefatus reverendissimus pater in aula manerii sui de Knoll predicti pro tribunali iudicialiter sedente, die et anno Domini immediate predictis, produci fecit contra prefatam Agnetem in negocio predicto ad convincendam eandem, in ipsius Agnetis presencia, Willelmum Riche de Benynden, Johannem Grebill senior, eiusdem Agnetis maritum, Johannem Grebill junior et Cristoferum Grebill, ipsius Agnetis filios naturales. Quos tunc ibidem iurari fecit ad sancta Dei evangelia – amore, timore, odio et favore postpositis – de dicendo omnem et meram veritatem quam sciverint de opinionibus dicte Agnetis contra fidem catholicam et sacramenta ecclesie. Presentibus tunc ibidem [. . .].

Presentation of their depositions and her reply to them. Ultimo die mensis Aprilis anno Domini supradicto, in capella manerii dicti reverendissimi patris de Knoll predicti, idem reverendissimus pater, pro tribunali ut superius iudicialiter sedens, presentibus tunc ibidem reverendo patre domino Johanne Sironenense episcopo ac venerabilibus viris magistris Cuthberto Tunstall, utriusque iuris, Roberto Wodward, decretorum, doctoribus, Gabrieli Silvester, sacre theologie professore, Roberto Ascom, et aliis, in presencia etiam magistrorum Thome Lawrence, Willelmi Potkyn et David Cooper, notariorum publicorum, publicavit dicta et deposiciones huiusmodi contra dictam Agnetem, ut prefertur, productorum et per eundem reverendissimum patrem secrete et singillatim examinatorum. Et dicta et deposiciones huiusmodi, in presencia dicte Agnetis, publice perlegi fecit. Et assignavit eidem Agneti, pro termino ad dicendum et proponendum omnia et singula que noverit contra huiusmodi testes et dicta eorundem que faciant pro defensione sua legitima, diem^q Veneris proximum. Que quidem Agnes tunc ibidem, post publicationem et lecturam prefatarum attestationum, publice et expresse negavit omnia et singula dicta testium predictorum et contradixit eisdem, dicens quod ipsi testes prodiderunt se et animas suas sic deponendo, et quod penitet eam ipsos filios suos umquam peperisse. Quorum testium dicta et depositiones sequuntur videlicet.

Deposition of John Grebill senior. John Grebill the elder of Tenterden, sworn and examyned of the tyme when his wif, Agnes, was first of the

---

^{q} *MS.* die.

errour ayenst the sacrament of the aulter, that it was but verey brede and not Crists body, flesshe and blood, he seith that first about the end of king Edwards daies the iiii^th in the house of this deponent by the teching of John Ive. And so furth from thens daiely tyll this tyme of detection she hath contynued. And besides that, whan his children Cristofer and John were about a vii yeres age, than this deponent taught theym the saide error ayenst the sacrament of the aulter in the presence of his said wif divers tymes in his owne house, she beyng alwayes of oon mynde in the said mysbelyve ayenst the sacrament of the aulter, that it was not Crists body, flesshe and bloode, but oonly brede. Examyned how he kneweth that she was stedfaste in the said error, for he saith that she alwayes withoute contradiccion affermed his teching and said the said opynion was goode and well contentid that hir children aforsaid were of the said opynyons ayenst the sacrament of the aulter.

Examyned also of the opynyon of his wif towching pilgremages, offeryngs and worshipping of seynts images, he saith that she in lykewise and at the same tyme whan John Ive and he taught hir of the said error ayenst the sacrament of the aulter, they taught hir also of the said opynions of pilgremages and worshipping of seynts ymages and offeryngs, that they were not in any wise to be kept nor profitable for mannys soule. The whiche errors she belived as this deponent saith, and yet beliveth as farre as he knoweth. Examyned how he knoweth that, he saieth that she alwayes affermed the same and that from hir first belive she never dide offer to seynts images nor yet wold goo to pilgremages. [fo. 171r] And divers tymes within his owne house in commenyng in the same errors ayenst pilgremages, offeryngs and worshipping of seynts images, contynually sithe hir first begynnyng till the season of this detection, his said wif in the presence of hym and his saide children John and Cristofer affermed the said opynions ayenst pilgrymages, offeryngs and worshipping of images and seynts to be good.

Examyned further of confession, how his wif belyved theryn, he saith that she beleved that confession made to a preest beyng the folowar of Peter and beyng pure and clene in life was good and profitable, and no confession was good that was made to a preest not beyng of clene life, for he had no power to assoyle any man of his synnes. And bothe he and his wif and his said children, Cristofer and John, were agreed togider by all the said tymes in his house never to make any confession of these aforsaid errors.

Examyned how the said Agnes belived of holy brede and holy water, he saith that she belyved that they were no better than other water and other brede. And in lykewise dud his sonnes by all the tyme abovesaid. Examyned how he knewe that, he saith that they brought home holy brede diverse tymes to his house and ete it, and had noon other regard unto it but as to other brede.

Also the whiche said opynions he saith that his said wif Agnes hath holden and belived sithe the said terme aboute the ende of kyng Edward the iiiith dayes till this tyme of deteccion. And within his house of Benynden divers tymes and specially the holydaies, she hath comyned and defended the said opinions in his presence and in the presence of his said ii sonnes, Cristofer and John.

Deposition of Christopher Grebill. Cristofer Grebill of Crainebroke, the son of John Grebill the elder of the age of xxii yeres, examyned the day and yere abovesaid and in the presence of the parties abovesaid of the bileve of his moder Agnes Grebill, specially first upon the sacrament of the aulter, item upon confession to a preest, item upon the sacrament of matrimony, item upon Cristenyng and bisshoppyng of children, item in goyng of pilgremage, worshippyng of seynts and offeryngs.

He aunswereth and saith that the said Agnes his moder held, belyved, taught and defendid that the sacrament of the aulter was but brede and not the very body of Criste, flesshe and bloode. And that baptisme was nothing worth, for a childe putt into the founte was no more the better than if he had be putt into other water. And that confirmacion ys a vayn thing and of noon effecte. And also that whan a man and a woman be contracted togider, it is not necessary to solemnise it in the churche. And yat the confession is sufficient to be made oonly to God and not to a preest. And over that, that goyng to pilgremage and offeryngs and worshipping of seynts ymages be not of any effecte nor to be doon. All the which said opinions and errours this Cristofer saith that his fader and also Agnes his moder hath taught, defended and hold and also manyteyned and commyned of theym within the house of his said fader, John Grebill the elder, divers tymes by the space of these iii yeres last passid as well in the holy daies as in the werken daies.

Examyned howe often tymes they did soo commyned togider, he saith he cannot tell the certeyntie of tymes. Examyned howe he knoweth that his fader and moder Agnes dide so belyve, he aunswereth and saith that whan they commyned togider of theym, then the said John his fader and Agnes his moder affermed and taught that they were goode and laufull and to be kept, holden and maynteyned. And agrement was made amongest theym that noon of theym shuld discovere nor bewray the other of thies belyves in any wise. Examyned by whom he was first induced into those errors, he saith that his fader and moder Agnes aforesaid taught this deponent and comyned divers tymes with this deponent in the said errors. But he saith that he hath no felyng in that maters of errors tyll he herd John Ive teche hym and till he sawe in John Ives books, which was by the space of thre yeres past.

Sith the whiche tyme the same deponent saith that he had communicacion with his saide fader and moder divers tymes in his saide faders house of the saide maters of errors, and at all tymes founde his saide fader and moder holding, maynteynyng and defending the same opinions and comfortyng hym in the same. And at some tyme was present with his saide fader and moder and hym in the same communicacion and in the saide house his broder John Grebill, which he thynketh belyved as they dide for he said nothing ayenst theym.

Deposition of John Grebill junior. John Grebill the yonger of Tenterden, xxi yeres of age, son of John Grebill and Agnes, sworn upon the evangelist the xxix day of Aprill and yere aforsaid by the said most reverend fader in God and in the presence of the saide wittnes, by vertue of his othe. Examyned how his moder hath and doeth belive of the sacrament of the aulter and goyng in pilgremages, offeryngs and worshipping of seynts images, he aunswereth and saith that in the house of his fader John Grebill in Benynden, often tymes as he resortid thider, his saide fader John Grebill and also his moder Agnes Grebill, beyng present also his brother Cristofer, taught, commyned, held and belived that the sacrament of the aulter was not Godds body, flesshe and bloode, but verey brede, wylling and advisyng hym to belyve in lykewise. And so he dide till he was detected.

Examyned how long tyme it is sithe they first so taught and counseilled hym, he saithe aboute xii months last past, and sithe that tyme divers dayes somtyme in the holydaies and somtyme in the werkyn daies as he resortid thider. At the whiche tymes the said John Grebill his fader and Agnes his moder taught and defendid as is abovesaid, saying that the sacrament of the aulter was but verey brede and not the body of Criste, and that they were not wise that otherwise wold belive. And in lykewise that pilgremages, offeryngs and worshipping of seynts images was not to be doon. And he saithe that he never herd his fader nor moder nor Cristofer his broder holdyng nor teching any other opinions then ys the saide errors ayenst the sacrament of the aulter and pilgremages, offeryngs and worshipping of seynts images, as ferre as he can remember. For he saith that his fader and moder forsaid taught hym and commyned with hym many tymes whan he was xiiii or xv yeres olde, and divers tymes sithens, but he never cowde perceyve their techings nor geve any hert therunto tyll this yere last past.

Deposition of William Ryche. William Ryche of Benynden, glover, of the age of xl yeres, sworn upon the holy evangelist by hym bodily[r]

---
[r] *MS.* boldly.

21

touched, the xxix daye of April, bifore the most reverend fader in God and wittenesses aforesaid. Examyned how he thynketh that Agnes Grebill, the wif of John Grebill the elder of Benynden, hath and doeth belyve in the sacrament of the aulter and other sacraments and teching of the churche, he aunswereth [fo. 171v] and saithe that she hath, and as he thynketh yet doeth, belive that the sacrament of the aulter ys but verey brede and not the body of Crist, flesshe and bloode. And also that the sacrament of matrimony is of noon effecte. Nor yet the sacrament of baptyme nor the sacrament of extreme unction ys nothing worthe. And more, that she damneth pilgremages, offerings and worshipping of seynts images.

Examyned howe he knoweth this, he aunswereth and saith that he hath ben divers tymes in the house of the said John Grebill at Benynden, and specially last at Barthilmewtyde[1] was xii moneths. At the whiche tyme, and divers other tymes bifore, this deponent commyned with the said John Grebill the elder in all the said errours and they togider held and belived as ys abovesaid, the said Agnes beyng present and heryng and consentyng to the same: and belyving as they dide that the sacrament of the aulter was not the body of Crist but verey brede and that the sacraments of matrimony, baptyme, confirmacion and extreme unccion, pilgremage goyng, offerings and worshipping of seynts images were not to be allowed but to be damned as nothing worth: beyng present no more at those communicacions at any tyme had in the said Grebills house at Benynden but the same John Grebill the elder, this deponent, and Agnes Grebill wif to the said John, and distrawght yong woman doughter to the said John and Agnes Grebill.

Her reply, and declaration of the sentence. Quo die Veneris, videlicet secundo die mensis Maii, anno Domini et loco immediate predictis, coram prelibato reverendissimo patre pro tribunali iudicialiter sedente, comparuit personaliter prefata Agnes Grebill, habens huiusmodi diem et locum ad dicendum contra testes, si velit. Que tunc et ibidem negavit omnes et singulas attestationes predictorum testium, dicens quod si et quatenus maritus et filii sui essent presentes et huiusmodi attestationes suas affirmarent, ipsa tamen negaret. Et exinde tunc ibidem introductis testibus predictis et personaliter constitutis, et dicta sua predicta contra ipsam Agnetem facie ad faciem affirmantibus, ipsa tamen omnino negavit et contradixit eisdem et nichil aliud pro se allegavit quare pro heretica pronunciari et declarari non debeat. Unde prefatus reverendissimus pater sentenciam contra eandem in huiusmodi negocio in scriptis tulit diffinitivam. Presentibus tunc ibidem reverendo patre

---

[1] The feast of St. Bartholomew was kept on 24 August.

22

domino Johanne Sironense episcopo, venerabilibus viris magistris
Cuthberto Tunstall, Thoma Welles, Clemente Browne, doctoribus
superius nominatis, ac notariis superius specificatis. Cuius sentencie
tenor sequitur videlicet.

Sentence. In[s] Dei nomine, Amen. Nos, Willelmus permissione divina
Cantuariensis archiepiscopus, totius Anglie primas et apostolice sedis
legatus, in quodam negocio heretice pravitatis contra te, Agnetem
Grebill nostre Cantuariensis diocesis ac nostre iurisdictioni notorie
subditam et subiectam, coram nobis in iudicio personaliter comparentem, nobis super heretica pravitate huiusmodi detectam et delatam ac
per nostram diocesim Cantuariensem antedictam notorie et publice in
ea parte apud bonos et graves diffamatam, ex officio nostro mero, rite
et canonice procedentes – auditis et intellectis, visis, cognitis
rimatisque ac matura deliberatione discussis et ponderatis dicti negocii
meritis, servatisque in omnibus et per omnia in eodem negocio de iure
servandis ac quomodolibet requisitis – pro tribunali sedentes, Christi
nomine invocato, et solum Deum pre oculis habentes.

Quia per acta, actitata, deducta, probata et exhibita coram nobis in
eodem negocio invenimus te per probationes legitimas coram nobis in
hac parte iudicialiter factas nonnullos et varios errores, hereses et
damnatas opiniones iuri divino et ecclesiastico obviantes, contrarios et
repugnantes contra fidem orthodoxam et universalem catholicam et
apostolicam ecclesiam determinatam et observatam tenuisse, credidisse, affirmasse, predicasse et dogmatisasse, et presertim contra
sacramenta altaris seu eucharistie et alia sacramenta et sancte matris
ecclesie dogmata. Et quatinus nos, Christi vestigiis inherendo, qui non
vult mortem peccatoris sed magis ut convertatur et vivat, sepe numero
conati fuimus te corrigere ac viis et modis licitis et canonicis, quibus
potuimus aut scivimus, ad fidem orthodoxam per universalem, catholicam et apostolicam ecclesiam determinatam et observatam ac ad
unitatem eiusdem sancte matris ecclesie reducere. Invenimus te adeo
dure[t] cervicis quod tuos errores et hereses huiusmodi nolueris sponte et
incontinenti confiteri, nec ad fidem catholicam et unitatem sancte
matris ecclesie antedictas debite reverti et redire. Sed tanquam
iniquitatis et tenebrarum filia in tantum indurasti cor tuum ut non velis
intelligere vocem tui pastoris tibi paterno compacientis affectu. Nec
velis piis et paternis monitionibus allici nec salubribus reduci
blandiciis.

Nos vero, nolentes quod tu que nequam es fias nequior, et gregem

---

[s] *Sentencia contra Agnetem Grebill* in margin.   [t] *MS.* duris.

23

dominicum in futurum tua heretice pravitatis labe de quo plurimum timemus inficias, idcirco, de consilio iurisperitorum nobis in hac parte assistentium cum quibus communicavimus in hac parte, te, Agnetem predictam, demeritis atque culpis per tuam damnabilem pertinaciam aggravatis, de et super huiusmodi detestabili heretice pravitatis reatu convictam et ad ecclesie unitatem penitencialiter redire nolentem, hereticam hereticisque credentem ac eorum fautarem et receptatricem pretextu premissorum fuisse et esse, cum dolore et amaritudine cordis indicamus et declaramus sentencialiter et diffinitive in his scriptis: relinquentes te ex nunc tanquam hereticam iudicio sive curie seculari. Teque Agnetem predictam, ut prefertur, hereticam nichilominus in maioris excommunicacionis sentenciam occasione premissorum incidisse et incurrisse, necnon excommunicatam[u] fuisse et esse pronunciamus, decernimus et declaramus etiam in hiis scriptis.

4. RELINQUISHING OF WILLIAM CARDER, AGNES GREBILL AND ROBERT
HARRYSON TO THE SECULAR ARM, 2 MAY, 1511 [fos. 172V–173R]

Excellentissimo^a principi et domino, domino Henrico¹ Dei gratia regi
Anglie et Francie et domino Hibernie illustrissimo, Willelmus permissione divina Cantuariensis archiepiscopus, totius Anglie primas et
apostolice sedis legatus: salutem in eo per quem reges regnant et
principes dominantur.

Vestre regie celsitudini tenore presentium significamus quod quidam
iniquitatis filii Willelmus Carder, Agnes Grebill et Robertus Haryson,
propter [fo. 173r] suos varios damnatos et manifestos errores et hereses
necnon opiniones damnabiles contra fidem catholicam et sanctam
matrem ecclesiam per eosdem et eorum quemlibet nonnullis modis et
mediis doctos et predicatos, per nos legitime et canonice convicti sunt
et heretici iudicati et eorum quilibet convictus et iudicatus est. Cum
igitur sancta mater ecclesia non habeat quod ulterius facere debeat in
hac parte, vestre regie celsitudini et brachio vestro seculari dictos
hereticos et eorum quemlibet relinquimus.

Datum in manerio nostro de Knoll secundo die mensis Maii anno
Domini millesimo quingentesimo undecimo et nostre translationis anno
octavo.

---

¹ King Henry VIII.

^a Certificatorium regie maiestati *in margin.*

25

(Ed.) N. TANNER

5. ABJURATIONS AND PENANCES OF CHRISTOPHER GREBILL, WILLIAM
RICHE OF BENENDEN, JOHN GREBILL SENIOR OF BENENDEN, JOHN
GREBILL JUNIOR OF TENTERDEN, WILLIAM OLBERD SENIOR
OF GODMERSHAM, AGNES IVE OF CANTERBURY, AGNES CHETYNDEN
OF CANTERBURY, THOMAS MANNYNG OF BENENDEN, JOAN COLYN
OF TENTERDEN AND ROBERT HILLES OF TENTERDEN, 2 TO 5 MAY, 1511
[fos. 159R–161V]

Heading. Nomina abiuratorum in crimine heretice pravitatis per
reverendissimum in Christo patrem et dominum, dominum Willelmum
permissione divina Cantuariensem archiepiscopum, totius Anglie
primatem et apostolice sedis legatum, et coram eodem, una cum actis
abiurationum suarum, anno Domini millesimo quingentesimo undecimo, sequuntur videlicet.

Appearance in court etc. Secundo die mensis Maii anno Domini
millesimo quingentesimo undecimo, coram reverendissimo in Christo
patre et domino, domino Willelmo permissione divina Cantuariense
archiepiscopo, totius Anglie primate et apostolice sedis legato, in
magna capella infra manerium suum de Knoll iurisdictionis sue
immediate pro tribunali iudicialiter sedente – presentibus reverendo
patre domino Johanne Dei gratia Sironense episcopo, magistris
Cuthberto Tunstall, utriusque iuris doctore, eiusdem reverendissimi
patris cancellario, Gabriele Silvester et Thoma Wellys, sacre theologie
professoribus, Roberto Wodwarde, decretorum doctore, Johanne
Aylove, in legibus bacallario, Thoma Baschurche,[1] capellano, Thoma
Laurence, Willelmo Potkyn et David Cooper, notariis publicis, et aliis –
comparuerunt personaliter Christoferus Grebill, Willelmus Riche,
Johannes Grebill senior de Benynden, Johannes Grebill junior,
Robertus Hilles parochie de Tenderden, Willelmus Olberde de
Godmersham Cantuariensis diocesis, Agnes Ive et Agnes Chetynden
parochie sancti Georgii civitatis Cantuariensis.

Et tunc ibidem nonnullis heresibus et erroribus suis in quibus se
fatebantur erravisse in specie, ac omnibus aliis et singulis erroribus et
heresibus contra fidem catholicam et ecclesie universalis determinationem in genere, renunciarunt et abiurarunt publice et solenniter iuxta
et secundum contenta in quibusdam scedulis suarum abiurationum
huiusmodi in anglicis conceptis et per eorum singulos singulariter
recitatis, et manibus suis signo crucis signatis: prestito primitus per
eosdem et eorum quemlibet de peragendo penitenciam eis et eorum
cuilibet per dictum reverendissimum patrem in ea parte iniungendam,

---

[1] See *BRUO*, i, 126, Thomas Baschurche.

ad sancta Dei evangelia per eorum singulos corporaliter tacta, iuramento corporali. Quarum scedularum tenores sequuntur videlicet.

Abjuration of Christopher Grebill. In[a] the name of God, Amen. Bifore you, the most reverend fader in God my lord William archibisshop of Caunterbury, I, Cristofer Grebill laymen of yor diocise of Canterbury, of my pure hert and free will confesse and knowlege that I in tymes past have beleved, thought, saide, holden, affermed and taught of the sacraments of the church and of the articles of the feith otherwise than the holy church of Rome and universall churche of God techeth, holdeth and observeth. And many and diverse open and damned errors and heresies contrary to the true and catholik feith and determinacion of holy churche I have bothe secretly and openly holden, beleved, affermed and taught. And specially among other, these errors and heresies folowyng, that is to wite.

First, that in the sacrament of the aulter is not the verey the body of Criste but materiall brede.

Also that the sacraments of baptism and confirmacion is not necessary nor profitable for mannys soule.

Also that confession of synnes ought not to be made to a preest.

Also that there is no more power geven by God to a preest than to a layman.

Also that solennisation of matrymony is not necessary nor profitable for the wele of mannys soule.

Also that the sacrament of extreme unction, called aneylyng, is not profitable nor necessary for mannys soule.

Also that pylgremages to holy and devoute places bee not profitable nother meritorious for mannys soule.

Also that images of seynts be not to be worshipped and that a man shulde pray to no seynt but oonly to God.

Also that holy water and holy brede be not the better after the benediccion made by the preest than it was before.

Wherefore I, the forseid Cristofer Grebill, willing hereaftir to beleve in the feith of Crist and of his churche and to folow the doctrine of holy churche, with a pure hert forsake and utterly despise my said errors, heresies and damnable opinions and confesse to be contraryuse and repugnaunt to the feith of Criste and determinacion of his holy churche. And the said errors, heresies and opinions in especiall and all other errors, heresies, fals doctrynes and damned opinions in generall likewise contrary and repugnant to the feith of Criste and of his church aforsaid I abjure, forsake and utterly renownce here bifore your

---

[a] Cristoferus Grebill *in margin.*

27

graciouse lordship and all the honourable audience here assembled.
And over that I swer by thies holy evangelies by me bodely here
touched that from hensforth I shall never holde, teche, bileve or
afferme the forsaid errors, heresies and damnable opinions nor noon
other ayenst the feith of Crists holy churche and determination of the
same. Nor yet I shall by myself or any other persone pryvatly or apertly
defende, maynteigne, socour, favor or supporte any persone that to my
knowlege holdeth, bileveth, affermeth or techeth any such errors,
heresies or damned opinions nor any persone that is suspect of the
same. And if I may knowe hereaftir any persone of suche errors,
heresies or any suche fals and damnable opinions suspecte, or any
persone holding or keping privay conventicles, assembles or fals
doctrynes or any opinions contrary to the comen doctryne of the church
aforesaid, or if I may knowe any of their fautors, comfortors,
consaillors or defensors, or any that have suspecte books or quayers of
any suche errors, heresies and damnable opinions, I shall without delay
geve knowlege unto yor goode lordship or unto the ordinary or
ordinaries of the same persones or ells unto yor and their successors. So
God me helpe and holy dome and thies holy evangelies.

In witnesse wherof to these presents with myn owne hand I have
made and subscribed the signe of the holy crosse. + Cristofer Grebill

Abjuration of William Riche. In[b] the name of God, Amen. Bifore you,
the moost reverend fader in God my lord William archibisshop of
Caunterbury, I, William Riche de Benynden of yor diocise of
Canterbury, of my pure hert and free will confesse and knowlege that I
in tymes past bifore this houre, that is to witte by the space of . . . [c]
yeres and more, have beleved, thought, said, holden, affermed and
taught of the sacraments of the churche and of the articles of the feith
otherwise than the holy churche of Rome and universall churche of
God techeth, holdeth and observeth. And many and dyvers open and
damned errors and heresies contrary to the true and catholike feith and
determynacion of holy church I have bothe secretly and openly holden,
bileved, affermed and taught. And specially among other, these errors
and heresies folowing, that is to witte.

First, that in the sacrament of the aulter is not the verey body of
Criste but oonly materiall brede.

Also that the sacraments of baptisme and confirmacion is not necessary nor profitable for mannys soule.

Also that confession of synnes ought not to be made to a prest.

Also that there ys no power geven by God to a prest more than to a
layman.

---

[b] Willelmus Riche *in margin.*   [c] *Blank space in MS.*

Also that the solennisacion of matrimony is not necessary nor profitable for the wele of mannys soule.

Also that the sacrament of extreme unction, callid aneylyng, is not profitable nor necessary for mannys soule.

Also that pilgrimages to holy and devoute places be not profitable nother meritoriouse for mannys soule.

Also that ymages of seynts be not to be worshipped and that a man shuld pray to no seynt but oonly to God.

Also that holy water and holy bredde be no better aftir the benediccion made by the preest than they were bifore.

[fo. 159v] Wherfore I, the forsaid William, willing hereafter to beleve in the feith of Criste and of his church and to folow the doctryne of holy churche, with a pure hert forsake and utterly despise my said errors, heresies and damnable opinions and confesse theym to be contrarious and repugnant to the feith of Criste and determinacion of his holy churche. And the said errours, heresies and opinions in especiall and all other errors, heresies, fals doctrynes and damned opinions in generall lykewise contrary and repugnannt to the feith of Criste and of his churche aforeseid I abjure, forsake and utterly renownce here tofore yor graciouse lordship and all the honorable audience here assembled. And over that I swer by thies evangelies by me bodily here touched yat from hensforth I shall never holde, teche, beleve or afferme the forsaid errors, heresies and damnable opinions nor noon other ayenst the feith of Crists holy churche and determinacion of the same. Nor yet I shall by myself or any other persone privatly or apertly defende maynteyne, socor, favor or support any persone that to my knowlege holdeth, beleveth, affermeth or techeth any suche errors, heresies or damned opinions nor any persone that is suspecte of the same. And if I may knowe hereaftir any persone of suche errors, heresies or of any suche fals and damned opinions suspecte or any persone holding or keping conventicles, assembles or fals doctrynes or any opinions contrary to the comen doctryne of the churche aforsaid, or if I may know any of their fautors, comfortors, counsaillors or defensours or any that have suspecte books or quayers of any suche errors, heresies and damnable opinions, I shall without delay geve knowlege unto your goode lordship or unto the ordinary or ordinaries of the same persones or ells unto yor and their officers. Soo God me helpe and holy dome and these holy evangelies.

In witness wherof to these presents with myn owne hande I have made and subscribed the signe of the holy cross +

Abjuration of John Grebill senior. In[d] the name of God, Amen. Byfore you, the most reverend fader in God my lord William archibisshop of

---

[d] Johannes Grebill senior *in margin.*

Caunterbury, I, John Grebill the elder of Benynden of your diocise of Caunterbury, of my pure hert and free will confesse and knowlege that I in tymes passed bifore this houre, that is to wite by the space of . . . ^e yeres and more, have beleved, thought, said, holden, affermed and taught of the sacraments of the church and of the articles of the feith otherwise than the holy church of Rome and universall church of God techeth, holdeth and observeth. And many and divers open and damned errors and heresies contrary to the true and catholike feith and determinacion of holy church I have bothe secretly and openly holden, bileved, affermed and taught. And specially among other, these errors and heresies folowing, that is to wite.

First that in the sacrament of the aulter ys not the verey body of Criste but oonly materiall brede.

Also that the sacraments of baptisme and confirmacion is not necessary nor profitable to mannys soule.

Also that confession of synnes ought not to be made to a preest.

Also that there is no more power geven by God to a preest than to a layman.

Also that the solennisacion of matrimony is not necessary nor profitable for the wele of mannys sowle.

Also that the sacrament of extreme unccion, callid aneylyng, is not profitable nor necessary for mannys sowle.

Also that pilgremages to holy and devoute places be not necessary nother meritorious for mannys soule.

Also that images of seynts be not to be worshipped and that a man shuld pray to no seynt but oonly to God.

And that holy water and holy brede is not the better aftir the benediccion made by the preest.

Wherfore I, the forsaid John, willing hereaftir to beleve in the feith of Criste and of his churche and to folowe the true doctryne of holy church, with a pure hert forsake and utterly despise my said errors, heresies and damnable opinions and confesse theym to be contraryous and repugnaunt to the feith of Criste and determinacion of his holy churche. And therfore the said errors, heresies and opinions in especiall and all other errours and heresies, fals doctrynes and damned opinions in generall likewise contrary and repugnaunt to the faith of Criste and determinacion of his church aforesaid I abjure, forsake and utterly renownce here bifore your graciouse lordship and all the honourable audience here assembled. And over that I swere by these holy evangelies by me bodily here touched that from hensforth I shall never holde, teche, beleve or afferme the forsaid errors, heresies and

---

^e *Blank space in MS.*

damnable opinions nor noon other ayenst the faith of Crists holy churche and determinacion of the same. Nor yet I shall by myself or any other persone pryvatly or apertly defende, maynteyne, socor, favor or support any persone that to[f] my knowlege holdeth, beleveth, affermeth or techeth any suche errors, heresies or damned opinions nor any persone that is suspect[g] of the same. And if I may knowe hereaftir any persone of suche errors, heresies or of any suche fals doctrynes or any opinions contrary to the comen doctryne of the church aforsaid, or if I may know any of their fautors, comfortors, conseillors or defensors or any that have suspect books or quayers of such errors, heresies and dampnable opinions, I shall without delay geve knowlege unto your goode lordship or unto the ordinary or ordynaries of the same persones or ells unto yor and their officers. Soo God me helpe and holy dome and thies holy evangelies.

In wittnes wherof to thise presents with myn owne hand I have made and subscribed the signe of the holy cross +

Abjuration of John Grebill junior. In[h] the name of God, Amen. Bifore you, the most reverend fader in God my lorde William archibisshop of Caunterbury, I, John Grebill the yonger of Tenterden of yor diocise of Caunterbury, of my pure hert and free wille confesse and knowlege that I in tymes passed bifore this houre, that is to witte by the space of . . . [i] yeres and more, have beleved, thought, said, holden, affermed and taught of the sacraments of the churche and of the articles of the feith otherwise than the holy churche of Rome and universall church of God techeth, holdeth and observeth. And many and divers open and damned errors and heresies contrary to the true and catholik feith and determinacion of holy churche I have bothe secretly and openly holden, beleved, affermed and taught. And specially among other, these errors and heresies folowing, that is to witte.

First, that in the sacrament of the aulter is not the verey body of Crist but oonly materiall brede.

Also that pilgremages to holy and devoute places be not necessary nother meritoriouse for mannys soule.

Also that images of seynts be not to be worshipped and that a man shuld praye to no seynt but oonly to God.

Wherfore I, the foresaid John, willing hereaftir to beleve in the feith of Crist and of his church and to folow the trewe doctryne of holy churche, with a pure hert forsake and utterly despise my said errors, heresies and damnable opinions and confesse theym to be contrariouse

---

[f] to *repeated.*   [g] *MS.* support.   [h] Johannes Grebill junior in *margin.*
[i] *Blank space in MS.*

31

and repugnant to the feith of Crist and determinacion of his holy churche. And therfore the said errors and opinions in especiall and all other errors and heresies, fals doctrynes and dampned opinions in generall likewise contrary and repugnant to the feith of Criste and determinacion of his church aforsaid I abjure, forsake and utterly renownce here bifore yor gracious lordship and all the honorable audience here assemblid. And over that I swere by thies holy evangelies by me bodely here touched that from hensforth I shall never hold, teche, beleve or afferme the forsaid errors, heresies and damnable opynions nor noon other ayenst the feith of Crists holy church and determynacion of the same. [fo. 160r] Nor yet I shall by myself or any other persone pryvatly or apartly defende, maynteyne, socor, favor or support any personne that to my knowlege holdeth, beleveth, affermeth or techeth any suche error, heresie or dampned opinion or any persone that is suspect of the same. And if I may knowe hereaftir any persone of suche error, heresie or of any suche fals doctrynes or any opinions contrary to the commen doctyne of the church aforesaid, or if I may know any of their fautors, comfortors, conseillors or defensors, or any that have suspect books or quayers of any suche errors, heresies and damnable opinions, I shall withoute delaye geve knowlege unto yor good lordship or unto the ordinary or ordinaries of the same persones or ells unto yor and their officers. Soo God me helpe and holy dome and thies holy evangelies.

In wittnes wherof to thies presents with myn owne hand I have made and subscribed the signe of the holy crosse +

Abjuration of William Olberd senior. In[j] the name of God, Amen. Bifore you, the most reverend fader in God my lord William archibisshop of Caunterbury, I, William Olberd the elder of the parisshe of Godmarsham of yor diocise of Caunterbury, of my pure hert and free will confesse and knowlege that in tymes passed bifore this houre, that is to wite by the space of . . . [k] yeres and more, have beleved, thought, saide, holden and affermed of the sacraments of the churche and of the articles of the faith otherwise than the holy church of Rome and universall church of God techeth, holdeth and observeth. And many and divers open and damned errors and heresies contrary to the true catholik faith and determynacion of holy church I have bothe secretly and openly holden, beleved, affermed and taught. And especially among other, thes errors and heresies folowing, that is to witte.

First, that in the sacrament of the aulter is not Crists very body but oonly materiall bred.

---

[j] Willelmus Olberd senior *in margin.*   [k] *Blank space in MS.*

Also that the sacraments of baptisme and confirmacion be not necessary nother profitable for mannys soule.

Also pilgrimages to holy and devoute places be not necessary nother
meritorious for the wele of mannys soule.

Also yat images of saynts be not to be worshiped and that a man
shuld pray to no seynt but oonly to God.

Wherfore I, the forsaid William Olberd, willing hereaftir to beleve in
the feith of Crist and of his churche and to folowe the true doctryne of
holy church, with a pure hert forsake and utterly despise my said errors
and damned opinions and confesse theym to be contraryous and repugnannt to the feith of Crist and determynacion of his holy churche
aforesaid. And therefore the said errors, heresies and opinions in
especiall and all other heresies and errors, fals doctrynes and damned
opinions in likewise contrary and repugnant to the feith of Criste and
determinacion of his churche aforesaid I abjure, forsake and utterly
renownce here bifore your gracious lordship and the honorable audience
here assembled. And over that I swere by thies holy evangelies by me
here bodely touched that from hensforth I shall never holde, teche, beleve
or afferme the foresaide errors, heresies and damnable opinions nor noon
other ayenst the feith of Crists holy church and determynacion of the
same. Nor yet I shall by myself or any other persone pryvatly or apartly
defende, maynteyne, socour, favor or supporte any persone that to my
knowlege holdeth, beleveth, affermeth or techeth any suche error, heresie
or damned opinion nor any persone that is suspecte of the same. And if I
may knowe hereaftir any persone of suche error, heresie or of any suche
damnable opinions suspecte, or any persones holding or keping privay
conventicles, assembles or fals doctrynes or any opinions contrary to the
comen doctryne of the churche aforesaid, or if I may knowe any of their
fautors, comfortors, consaillors or defensors or any that hath suspect
books or quayers of any suche errors, heresies or damnable opinions, I
shall without delaye geve knowlege unto yor good lordship or unto the
ordinary or ordinaries of the same persones or ellys unto yor and their
officers. So God my helpe and holy dome and thies hóly evangelies.

In wittnes wherof to thies presentes with myn owne hand I have
made and subscribed the signe of the holy crosse +

Abjuration of Agnes Ive of Canterbury. In[1] the name of God, Amen.
Bifore you, the most reverend fader in God my lord William
archibisshop of Caunterbury, I, Agnes Ive of yor citie of Canterbury, of
my pure hert and free will confesse and knowlege that I in tymes past
bifore this houre, that is to wite by the space of . . .[m] and more, have

---

[1] Agnes Ive *in margin.*   [m] *Blank space in MS.*

beleved, thought, said, holden, affirmed and taught of the sacraments of the churche and of the articles of the faith otherwise than the holy church of Rome and universall churche of God techeth, holdeth and observeth. And many divers open and damned errors and heresies contrarie to the true and catholike faith and determynacion of holy churche I have bothe secretly and openly holden, beleved, affermed and taught. And specially among other, these errors and heresies folowing, that is to witte.

First that in the sacrament of the aulter is not the verey body of Crist but oonly materiall bred.

Also that the sacraments of baptisme and confirmacion is not necessary nor profitable to mannys soule.

Also that confession of synnes ought not to be made to a preest.

Also there is no more power geven by God to a preest than to a layman.

Also that the sacrament of extreme unccion, callid aneyling, is not profitable nor necessary for mannys soule.

Also that pilgremages to holy and devoute places be not necessary nor meritoriouse for mannys soule.

Also that images of seynts be not to be worshipped and that a man shuld pray to no seynt but oonly to God.

Also that holy water and holy bred is not the better aftir the benediccion made by the preest.

Wherfore I, the forsaid Agnes, willyng hereaftir to beleve in the faith of Crist and of his churche and to folowe the true doctryne of holy churche, with a pure hert forsake and utterly despise my said errors, hereies and damnable opinions and confesse theym to be contraryous and repugnaunt to the faith of Crist and the determinacion of his holy church. And therfore the said errors, heresies and opinions in especiall and all other errors and heresies, fals doctrines and dampned opinions in generall likewise contrary and repugnant to the faith of Criste and determinacion of his churche aforsaid I abjure, forsake and utterly renownce here bifore yor gracious lordship and all the honorable audience here assembled. And over that I swere by thies holy evangelies by me bodely here touched that from hensforth I shall never holde, teche, beleve or afferme the forsaid errors, heresies and damnable opinions nor noon other ayenst the faith of Crists holy church and determinacion of the same. Nor yet I shall by myself or any other persone pryvatly or apartly defende, maynteyne, socor or support any persone that to my knowlege holdeth, beleveth, affermeth or techeth any suche errors, heresie or dampned opinions nor any persone yat is suspecte of the same. And if I may knowe hereaftir any persone of suche errors, heresis or of any suche fals doctrynes or any opinions contrary to the commen doctryne of the churche aforsaid, or if I may knowe any of their fautors, comfortors, counsaillors or defensors or any that have suspect books or quayers or suche errors, heresies and damnable opinions, I shall withoute delaye geve knowlege unto yor good lordshipp, yor successors or unto the ordynarie or ordinaries of the same persones or ells unto yor and their officers. So God me help and holy dome and thies holy evanglies.

In wittnes wherof to thise presents with myn owne hand I have made and subscribed the signe of the holy crosse +

Abjuration of Agnes Chetynden. In[n] the name of God, Amen. Bifore you, the moost reverend fader in God my lord William archibisshop of Caunterbury, I, Agnes Chetynden of yor citie of Caunterbury, of my pure hert and free will confesse and knowlege that I in tymes past bifore this houre, that is to wite by the space of . . . [o] yeres and more, have bileved, thought, said, holden, affermed and taught of the sacraments of the church and of the articles of the faith otherwise than the holy church of Rome and universall church of God techeth and observeth. And many and divers open and damned errors and heresies contrary to the true and catholik faith and determinacion of holy churche I have bothe secretly and openly hold, beleved, affermed and taught. And specially among other, thies errors and heresies folowing, that is to say.

First, that in the sacrament of the aulter [fo. 160v] is not the verey body of Criste but oonly materiall bredde.

Also that pilgremages to holy and devoute places be not necessary ne meritorious for mannys soule.

Also that images of seynts be not to be worshipped and that a man shuld pray to no seynt but oonly to God.

Wherfore I, the said Agnes, willing hereaftir to bileve in the faith of Criste and of his churche and to folow the true doctryne of holy churche, with a pure hert forsake and utterly despise my said errours, heresies and damnable opinions and confesse theym to be contraryous and repugnaunt to the faith of Criste and determinacion of his holy churche. And therfore the said errors, heresies and damned opinions in especiall and all other errors and heresies, fals doctrines and damned opinions in generall likewise contrarye and repugnaunt to the faith of Criste and determinacion of his churche aforsaid I abjure, forsake and utterly renownce here bifore your gracious lordship and all the honorable audience here assembled. And over that I swere by thies holy evangelies by me here bodily touched that from hensforth I shall never holde, teche, beleve or afferme the forsaid errors, heresies and

---

[n] Agnes Chetynden *in margin.*   [o] *Blank space in MS.*

damnable opinions nor noon other ageinst the feith of Crists holy churche and determinacion of the same.

Nor yet I shall by myself or any other persone pryvatly or apertly defende, maynteyne, socour and support any persone that to my knowlege holdeth, beleveth, affermeth and techeth any suche errors, heresies or damned opinions nor any persone that is suspecte of the same.

And if I may knowe hereafter any persone of suche error, heresie or of any suche fals doctrynes or any opinions contrary to the commen doctryne of the churche aforsaid, or if I may know any of their fautors, comfortors, concelors or defensors or any that have suspecte books or quayers of suche errors, heresies and damnable opinions, I shall withoute delaye geve knowlege unto your goode lordship or unto the ordinarye or ordinaries of the same persones or ells unto yor and their officers. So God help me and holy dome and thies holy evangelies.

In wittnes wherof to these presents with myn owne hand I have made and subscribed the signe of the holy crosse +

Absolution from excommunication and penances. Et deinde idem reverendissimus pater eosdem a sentencia excommunicationis, quam premissorum pretextu incurrerunt, absolvit et sacramentis ecclesie ac communioni fidelium restituit. Et tunc ibidem in partem penitencie primo iniunxit eisdem et eorum singulis quod confiteantur se sacerdoti et recipiant eucharistiam; item quod eant ad videndum Willelmum Carder ignem passurum propter suam incorrigibilitatem. Et insuper tunc ibidem idem reverendus pater assignavit eisdem diem Lune proxime ex tunc sequentem, hora octava ante meridiem, ad recipiendam reliquam partem penitencie sue.

Appearance in court etc. Prefato secundo die mensis Maii, hora tercia post meridiem, in quodam oratorio dicti reverendissimi patris et domini, domini Willelmi permissione divina Cantuariensis archiepiscopi, totius Anglie primatus et apostolice sedis legati, infra manerium suum de Knoll predictum, presentibus tunc ibidem magistris Cuthberto Tunstall, utriusque iuris, Gabriele Silvester, sacre pagine, Roberto Wodwarde, decretorum, Roberto Cooper,[2] musica, doctoribus, Johanne Aylove, in legibus baccalario, dominis Thoma Baschusche et Philippo Mesmer, capellanis, comparuerunt coram reverendissimo patre iudicialiter sedente Thomas Mannyng de Benynden et Johanna Colyn nuper de Tenterden. Et modo quo supra abiurarunt et renunciarunt et eorum uterque sic abiuravit et renunciavit omnibus heresibus et erroneis opinionibus suis per eos confessatis in specie, et omnibus aliis

[2] See *BRUC*, 164–5, Robert Cooper.

in genere contra fidem catholicam et universalis ecclesie determin-acionem faciendis, iuxta contenta in scedulis abiurationum suarum huiusmodi manibus suis signatis signo crucis et per eosdem publice recitatis: prestito primitus per eosdem et eorum utrumque de peragendo penitenciam eis et eorum utroque per dictum reverendissimum patrem in ea parte iniungendam, ad sancta Dei evangelia per eorum singulos corporaliter tacta, iuramento corporali. Quarum scedularum tenores sequuntur videlicet.

Abjuration of Thomas Mannyng. In[p] the name of God, Amen. Bifore you, the moost reverend fader in God my lorde William archibisshop of Caunterbury, I, Thomas Mannyng of Benynden of your diocise of Caunterbury, of my pure hart and free will confesse and knowlege that I in times past bifore this houre, that is to witte by the space of . . . [q] yeres and more, have beleved, saide, thought, holden, affermed and taught of the sacraments of the churche and of the articles of the feith otherwise than the holy churche of Rome and universall churche of God techeth, holdeth and observeth. And many and diverse open and damned errors and heresies contrarie to the true and catholike feith and determynacion of holy churche I have bothe secretly and openly holden, beleved, affermed and taught. And specially among other, these errors and heresies folowing, that is to witte.

First that in the sacrament of the aulter is not the verey body of Criste but oonly materiall brede.

Also that the sacraments of baptisme and confirmacion is not necessary nor profitable to mannys soule.

And that confession of synnes ought not to be made to a preest.

Also that there is no power geven by God to a preest more than to a layman.

Also that solennisacion of matrimony is not necessarie nor profitable for the wele of mannys soule.

And that the sacrament of extreme unccion, callid anelyng, ys not profitable nor necessary for mannys soule.

Also that pilgremages to holy and devoute places be not profitable nother meritoriouse for mannys soule.

Also that images of seynts be not to be worshipped and that a man shuld praye to no seynt but oonly to God.

Also that holy water and holy brede be no bettir aftir the benediccion made by the preest than they were bifore.

Wherfore I, the said Thomas, willing hereaftir to beleve in the feith of Criste and of his churche and to folowe the doctryne of holy churche, with a pure hert forsake and utterly despise my said errors, heresies and

---

[p] Thomas Mannyng *in margin.*   [q] *Blank space in MS.*

damnable opinions and confesse them to be contrarious and repugnaunt to the faith of Criste and determinacion of his holy churche. And the saide errors, heresies and opinions in especiall and all other errors, heresies, fals doctrynes and damned opinions in generall likewise contrary and repugnaunt to the feith of Criste and of his churche aforsaid I abjure, forsake and utterly renownce here bifore your graciouse lordship and all the honorable audience here assembled. And over that I swere by thies evangelies by me bodly here touched that from hensforth I shall never hold, teche, beleve or afferme the forsaid errors, heresies and damnable opinions nor noon other ayenst the feith of Crists holy churche and determinacion of the same. Nor yet I shall by myself or any other persone pryvatly or apertly defende, maynteyne, socour, favor or supporte any persone that to my knowlege holdeth, beleveth, affermeth or techeth any suche errors, heresies or damned opinions nor any persone that is suspecte of the same. And if I may knowe hereaftir any persone of suche errors, heresies or of any suche fals or damned opinions suspecte or any persone holding or keping privay conventicles, assembles or fals doctrynes or any opinions contrary to the commen doctryne of the churche aforsaid, or and if I may knowe any of theire fautors, confortors, consaillors or defensors or any that have suspect books or quayers of any suche errors, heresies and damnable opinions, I shall withoute delay geve knowlege unto yor goode lordship or unto the ordinary or ordinaryes of the same persone or ells unto yor and their officers. So God me helpe and holy dome and thies holy evangelies.

In wittnes wherof to these presents with myn owne hand I have made and subscribed the signe of the holy crosse +

Abjuration of Joan Colyn. In[r] the name of God, Amen. Bifore you, the most reverent fader in God my lord William archibisshop of Caunterbury, I, Johane Colyn of Tenterden of yor diocise of Caunterbury, of my pure hert and free will confesse and knowlege that I in tymes past have beleved, thought, said, holden, affermed and taught of the sacraments of the church and of the articles of the feith otherwise than the holy churche of Rome and universall churche of God techeth, holdeth and observeth. And many and diuerse open and damned errors and heresies contrary to the true and catholike feith and determynacion of holy churche I have bothe secretely and openly holden, beleved, affermed and taught. And specially among other, these errors and heresies folowing, that is to witte.

Furst that the sacraments of baptisme and confirmacion is not necessary nor profitable to mannys soule.

---

[r] Johanna Colyn *in margin.*

Also that the solennisacion of matrimonye is not necessary nor profitable for the wele of mannys soule.

Also that pilgremages to holy and devoute places be not necessary nother [fo. 161r] meritoriouse for mannys soule.

Also that images of seynts be not to be worshipped and that a man shuld praye to no seynt but oonly to God.

Also that holy water and holy brede is not the better aftir the benediccion made.

Wherfor I, the forsaid Johane, willing heraftir to beleve in the faith of Criste and of his church and to folowe the doctrine of holy church, with a pure hert forsake and utterly despise my said errors, heresies and damnable opinions and confesse theym to be contrariouse and repugnaunt to the faith of Criste and determinacion of his holy churche. And the said errors, heresies and opinions in especiall and all other errors, heresies, false doctrynes and damned opinions in generall likewise contrary and repugnaunt to the faith of Criste and of his churche aforsaid I abjure, forsake and utterly renownce here bifore yor gracious lordship and all the honorable audience here assembled. And over that I swer by thies holy evangelies by me bodily here touched that from hensforth I shall never hold, teche, beleve or afferme the forsaid errors, heresies and damnable opinions nor noon other ayenst the feith of Crists holy churche and determinacion of the same. Nor yet I shall by myself or any other persone pryvatly or apertly defende, maynteyn, socor, favor or supporte any persone that to my knowleche holdeth, beleveth, affermeth or techeth any suche errors, heresies or damned opinions nor any persone that is suspecte of the same. And if I may knowe hereaftir any persone of suche errors, heresies or of any suche fals and damned opinions suspect or any persone holding or keping privay conventicles, assembles or fals doctrynes or any opinions contrary to the commen doctyne of the church aforsaid, or if I may know any of their fautours, confortors, concelors and defensors or any that have suspect books or quayers of any suche errors, heresies and damned opinions, I shall withoute delaye geve knowlege unto yor goode lordship or unto the ordinary or ordinaries of the same persones or ells unto yor and their officers. So God me[s] helpe and holy dome and thies holy euangelies.

In wittnes whereof to these presents with myn owne hand I have made and subscribed the signe of the holy crosse +

Penances. Quo die Lune adveniente, videlicet quinto mensis Maii predicti, loco quo supra, presentibus testibus supranominatis, idem

[s] *MS.* me.

39

reverendissimus pater, iudicialiter pro tribunali sedens, iniunxit Cristofero Grebill, Roberto Hilles, Willelmus Riche, Willelmo Olberd seniori, Agneti Ive et Johanni Grebill seniori penitenciam infrascriptam videlicet.

In primis quod quilibet eorum gestabit fasciculum depictum cum rubeis coloribus mixtis et circumdatis in modum flamme ignis circumposite – videlicet, masculi sinistro humero ex parte exteriori in sinistra manica vestimenti sui superioris, et femine in sinistra manica huiusmodi vestimenti sui superioris – publice absque aliqua occultatione durante vita eorum cuiuslibet, nisi aliter fuerit per eundem reverendissimum patrem aut suos successores cum eisdem in ea parte dispensatum.

Item quod eorum quilibet in foro civitatis Cantuarie in Sabbato proxime tunc futuro, et in Dominica proxima ex tunc proxime sequente in ecclesia cathedrali Christi Cantuariense ante processionem, gestabit fasciculum ligneum in humero suo. Et ibidem intererit eorum quilibet sermoni ibidem fiendo, cum huiusmodi fasciculo in humero suo, quousque sermo finiatur. Et die Dominica proxime sequente quilibet huiusmodi abiuratorum gestabit simile fasciculum ligneum modo consimili ante processionem in ecclesiis suis parochialibus. Et premissa facient nudi caput, tibias et pedes.

Item quod in nullo alio loco deinceps manebit eorum aliquis extra parochias ubi nunc inhabitant, nisi prius a dicto reverendissimo patre aut eius succesoribus licentiam expressam obtinuerit.

Item si quos heretice pravitatis libros habuerit, eosdem dicto reverendissimo patri indilate apportabit.

Item si quos de heresi suspectos aut libros heretice pravitatis habentes in presenti noscunt aut in futurum noscent, de nominibus suspectorum et huiusmodi libros habentium prefatum reverendissimum patrem sine dilatione certiorem efficient.

Item quod diebus Dominicis et festivis eorum quilibet frequentabit ecclesiam suam parochialem et ibidem divina audiet, ut bonus Christianus.

Et insuper monuit eosdem ad perimplendam huiusmodi penitenciam et quamlibet partem eiusdem sub pena relapsus.

Item idem reverendissimus pater iniunxit tunc ibidem Thome Mannyng et Johanni Grebill junior quod die Dominica proxima eorum uterque in ecclesia sua parochiali antecedet processionem gestantes fasciculum ligneum, et post processionem illud ibidem relinquant.

Appearance in court, etc. Eisdem quinto die mensis Maii et loco immediate predicto in presentia supradicta, coram eodem reverendissimo patre pro tribunali adhuc sedente iudicialiter, comparens personaliter Robertus Hilles de Tenterden et publice adiuravit et renunciavit omnibus heresibus et damnatis opinionibus suis, iuxta contenta in quadam scedula abiurationis sue huiusmodi per eum publice recitata tunc ibidem et signo crucis manu sua signata: prestito per eundem Robertum, ad sancta Dei evangelia per eum corporaliter tacta, de perimplendo penitenciam sibi ob premissa per eundem reverendissimum patrem iniungendam iuramento corporali. Cuius scedule tenor sequitur videlicet.

Abjuration of Robert Hilles. In[t] the name of God, Amen. Bifore you, the moost reverend fader in God my lorde William archebisshop of Caunterbury, I, Robert Hilles of Tenterden of your diocise of Caunterbury, of my pure hert and fre will confesse and knowlege that I in tymes passed bifore this houre, that is to witte by the space of xii yeres and more, have beleued, thought, said, holden, affermed and taught of the sacraments of the church and of the articles of the faith otherwise than the holy church of Rome and univesall churche of God techeth, holdeth and obserueth. And many and divers open and damned errors and heresies contrarie to the true and catholik feith and determinacion of holy churche I have secretly and openly holden, beleved, affermed and taught. And specially among other, thies errors and heresies folowing, that is to witte.

Furst, that in the sacrament of the aulter is not the verey body of Criste but oonly materiall bred.

Also that confession of synnes ought not to be made to a preest.

Also that there is no more power geven by God to a preest than to a layman.

Also that the solennisacion of matrymony is not necessary nor profitable for the wele of mannys soule.

And that the sacrament of extreme unccion, callid aneylyng, is not profitable nor necessary for mannys soule.

Also that pilgremages to holy and devoute places be not necessary nother meritoriouse for a mannys soule.

Also that images of seynts be not to be worshipped and that a man shuld pray to no seynt but oonly to God.

Also that holy water and holy brede is not the better aftir the benediccion made by the preest.

Wherefore I, the forsaid Robert Hilles, willing hereaftir to beleve in the faith of Crist and of his church and to folowe the true doctryne of holy churche, with a pure hert forsake and utterly despise by said errors, heresies and damnable opinions and confesse theym to be contrarious and repugnaunt to the feith of Crist and determinacion of

---

[t] Robertus Hilles *in margin.*

holy churche. And therfore the said errours, heresies and opinions in especiall and all other errours and heresies, fals doctrynes and damned opinions in generall lykewise contrary and repugnaunt to the faith of (fo. 161v) Criste and determinacion of his church aforsaid I abjure, forsake and utterly renownce here bifore youre gracious lordship and all the honourable audience here assembled. And over that I swere by these holy evangelies by me bodely here touched that from hensforth I shall never holde, teche, beleve or afferme the forsaid errors, hereies and damnable opinions nor noon other ayenst the feith of Crists holy church and determinacion of the same. Nor yet I shall by myself or any other persone privatly or apertly defende, maynten, socor, favor or support any persone that to my knowlege holdeth, beleveth, affermeth or techeth any suche errors, heresies or damned opynion or any persone that is suspect of the same. And if I may know hereaftir any persone of suche error, heresie or of any suche fals doctryne or any opinions contrary to the commen doctrine of the church aforesaid, or if I may knowe any of their fautors, comfortors, concelors or defensors or any that have suspect bookes or quayers of suche errors, heresies and damnable opinions, I shall withoute delay geve knowlege unto yor good lordship or unto yor ordinary or ordinaryes of the same persones or ells unto yor and thier officers. So God me help and holy dome and thies holy evangelies.

In wittnes wherof to thies presents with myn owne hand I have made and subscribed the signe of the holy crosse +

Penances. Item tunc ibidem idem reverendissimus pater iniunxit Johanne Colyn quod post hec neminem celabit quem noverit de heresi suspectum seu heresim docentem aut tenentem; et quod non amovebit se ad alia loca, morandi causa, nisi prius certificabit eundem reverend-issimum patrem aut suos successores de loco ubi manebit; et quod non comedet carnes aliquo die Mercurii per annum integrum proxime futurum.

6. PROCEEDINGS AGAINST JOHN BROWNE[1] OF ASHFORD, 8 TO 19 MAY, 1511
[fos. 173R–174R]

His appearance in court. Octavo die mensis Maii anno Domini millesimo quingentesimo undecimo in capella manerii reverendissimi patris et domini Willelmi, permissione divina Cantuariensis archiepiscopi, totius Anglie primatis et apostolice sedis legati, de Lamehith coram eodem reverendissimo patre pro tribunali iudicialiter sedente, presentibus et assidentibus eidem venerabilibus viris magistris Johanne Colet,[2] sacre theologie professore, decano ecclesie cathedralis sancti Pauli Londoniensis, Thoma Wodyngton,[3] decretorum doctore, curie Cantuariensis officiali, Cuthberto Tunstall, utriusque iuris, Thoma Perte,[4] legum, Gabrieli Silvestre, sacre pagine, doctoribus, comparuit personaliter Johannes Browne de Assheford Cantuariensis diocesis. Quem idem reverendissimus pater iurare fecit ad sancta Dei evangelia de fideliter respondendo certis articulis contra eum in negocio heretice pravitatis ex officio dicti reverendissimi patris ministratis. Quorum articulorum tenores sequuntur videlicet.

Charges against him. In[a] Dei nomine, Amen. Nos, Willelmus permissione divina Cantuariensis archiepiscopus, totius Anglie primas et apostolice sedis legatus, tibi, Johanni Browne de Assheford nostre Cantuariensis diocesis ac nostre iurisdictioni notorie subdito et subiecto, ad meram anime tue correctionem necnon ad omne iuris effectum qui exinde sequi poterit aut debebit, obiicimus et articulamur coniunctim et divisim omnes et singulos articulos infrascriptos ac quamlibet partem et particulam eorundem, mandantes et precipientes quatinus eisdem omnibus et singulis singulariterque in eisdem contentis plenam, meram et nudam respondeas veritatem sub pena iuris.

In[b] primis tibi obiicimus et articulamur quod tu fuisti et es nostre Cantuariensis diocesis ac nostre iurisdictioni notorie subditus et subiectus.

Item[c] quod tu per plures annos elapsos omnes et singulos hereses, errores et damnatas opiniones subsequentes seu saltem eorum aliquos credidisti, docuisti, tenuisti, affirmasti et predicasti, videlicet.

Quod in sacramento altaris sive eucharistie non est verum corpus Christi sed panis materialis.

---

[1] For an account of his arrest, trial and death, which John Foxe said had been related to him by Browne's daughter Alice, see Foxe, *Acts* (Ed. Pratt), iv, 181–2 and 722–3.

[2] John Colet, Dean of St. Paul's cathedral, London, 1505–19.

[3] See *BRUO*, iii, 2083, Thomas Woodington.

[4] See *BRUC*, 451, Thomas Perte.

---

[a] Johannes Browne *in margin.*   [b] i *in margin.*   [c] ii *in margin.*

43

Item^d quod sacramenta baptismi et confirmacionis non sunt necessaria ad salutem anime.

Item^e quod vocalis, auricularis sive verbalis confessio peccatorum non est facienda sacerdoti.

Item^f quod nulla potestas fuit aut est sacerdotibus a Deo collata^g magis quam laicis in sacramentis ecclesie ministrandis, missis celebrandis aut aliis divinis officiis exequendis.

Item^h quod matrimonii solennisacio non est necessaria ad anime salutem nec a iure divino instituta.

Itemⁱ quod sacramentum extreme unctionis non est utile aut necessarium ad anime salutem.

Item^j quod imagines sancte crucis et crucifixi ac beate Marie virginis et aliorum sanctorum nullo modo sunt venerande, sed quod venerantes huiusmodi imagines committunt idolatriam.

Item^k quod peregrinaciones ad loca sancta et devota, ubi solet populus christianus sanctos et reliquias sanctorum venerari, non sunt necessarie sive meritorie ad salutem anime sed damnabiles, detestando huiusmodi peregrinationes ad huiusmodi loca reprehendendo, dicendo huiusmodi peregrinantes sic peregrinando committere idolatriam.

Item^l quod oraciones non sunt effundende ad sanctos sed ad solum Deum, qui solus audit orantes.

Item^m quod panis benedictus et aqua benedicta non sunt maioris virtutis et efficacie post benedictionem factam a sacerdote quam ante benedictionem.

Itemⁿ quod tu omnes et singulos hereses, errores et damnatas opiniones supradictas seu eorum aliquos credis, doces, tenes, affirmas et predicas etiam in presenti.

Item^o quod tu omnia et singula premissa timore probationum solum et ad evadendam penam es confessus. Et si detecta per alios non fuissent nec timeres te posse convinci per testes, casu quo illa negares premissa numquam sponte confessus fuisses. Nec ea nunc sponte sed timore probationum confiteris.

Item^p quod tu cum aliis personis de prefatis heresibus, erroribus et damnatis opinionibus secum communicantibus sepius et iteratis vicibus communicasti. Et ut quod habuisti et habes libros concernentes dictos errores.

His reply to the charges. Qui quidem Johannes Browne, tunc ibidem examinatus et interrogatus de et super articulis huiusmodi, fatetur se

---

^d iii *in margin.*   ^e iiii *in margin.*   ^f v *in margin.*   ^g *MS.* collatis.   ^h vi *in margin.*
ⁱ vii *in margin.*   ^j viii *in margin.*   ^k ix *in margin.*   ^l x *in margin.*
^m xi *in margin.*   ⁿ xii *in margin.*   ^o xiii *in margin.*   ^p xiiii *in margin.*

fuisse et esse iurisdictionis dicti reverendissimi patris. Reliquos articulos omnes et singulos publice tunc ibidem negavit.

The witnesses. Et deinde tunc ibidem prefatus reverendissimus pater produci fecit in testes contra dictum Johannem Browne, ad convincendum eundem, Thomam Harwode de Rowenden, Johannam Harwode eius uxorem, Philippum Harwode de eadem et Willelmum Baker de . . . ᵠ. Et eosdem, in presencia dicti Johannis Browne, ad sancta Dei evangelia iurare fecit dicendo veritatem quam noverint de opinione dicti Johannis contra catholicam fidem et ecclesie universalis determinationem. Qui quidem testes sic iurati et in forma iuris examinati deposuerunt prout sequitur videlicet.

Deposition of Joan Harwode. Johane Harwode, the wif of Thomas Harwode de Rowenden of the diocise of Caunterbury, sworne and examyned upon the bileve of John Browne of Assheford, cutler, in the sacraments of the church and the articles of the faith, she saith and deposith that about Cristmas, was vi or vii yeres, the said John Browne came to the house of the husband of this deponent. And then and there yn an evenyng sittyng by the fyre in the hall hir said husbond, John Browne and this deponent hadde communicacion ayenst the sacrament of the aulter. And then and there they three togider concluded, affermed, held and beleved that the sacrament of the aulter was not the body of Crist, flesshe and bloode, but oonly brede. And then and there as well the said John Browne as hir said husbond commaunded and charged this deponent never to utter to any persone upon payne of hir lif of their forsaid communicacion ayenst the sacrament of the aulter, everyche of theym saying that it shuld cost theym all their lyves and be brentʳ if it were uttred.

Also this deponent saith that aboute Shroftede,⁵ was iii or iiii yeres past, this deponent and hir said husbond went unto the house of the said John Browne in Assheford, where and when this deponent, hir said husbond and the said John Browne sittyng all togider there by the fyre, etyng and drynkyng, had communicacion ayenst worshipping of images of seyntsˢ and goyng on pilgremage. Than and there Elizabeth, the wif of John Browne, beyng present at the said communicacion, concluded, helded, beleved and affermed and everyche of theym concluded, helded, beleved and affermed that goyng on pilgremage was nothing ellys but to spendᵗ money in waste, better then to goo on pilgremage; and that worshipping of images of our Lady and other seynts was not to be doon, for our Lady

---

⁵ Shrove Tuesday fell on 7 March in 1508, 16 February in 1507.

ᵠ *Blank space in MS.*   ʳ and *follows* brent.   ˢ *MS.* seynt.   ᵗ *MS.* spent.

and all seynts were in heven and therfore their ymages shuld not be worshipped in erthe; and that it advayled not to offer or sett upp a candill bifore any images in churches, saying that it was nothing worthe.

Deposition of William Baker. William Baker, sworne and examyned upon the opinions of John Browne ayenst the sacraments of the churche, saith that upon our Lady day callid the Anunciacion[6] last past, was xii moneths, in a garden at Charte – but who owneth the garden he cannot tell – this deponent and John Browne had communicacion todiger of the prayers of purgatory. And then and there the said John Browne said that there was no purgatory but [fo. 173v] oonly in this world, and aftir that a man was decessid he shulde goo streight to heven or to hell. Atte whiche tyme he saith that they had noon other communicacion there.

Also this deponent saith that upon seynt Dunstons daye[7] last paste, in the house of this deponent, the said John Browne, Thomas Mannyng and this deponent had communicacion ayenst the sacrament of the aulter. And then and there the said Browne said that the sacrament of the aulter, that the preest helde betwene his hands, was not the body of Criste, flesshe and bloode, but oonly brede. And so the said John Browne [and] Thomas Mannyng then and there and everyche of them helde, beleved and affermyd. And furthermore the said John Browne than and there said that they shuld trust to God in heven and trust not to that no moo then beyng present, as he remembreth.

Also this deponent saith about Cristmas last past, as he remembreth, betwix the house of this deponent and a chapell callid Mylkehouse within the parisshe of Crainebroke, as this deponent and the said Browne walked by the waye, the said John Browne said unto this deponent that worshipping of images and goyng on pilgremage was but idolatrye: no moo then beyng present.

Deposition of Thomas Harwode. Thomas Harwode of Rowenden, lxxiiii yeres of age, sworne and examyned upon the beleve of John Browne of Assheford ayenst the sacraments of the churche, saith that upon a Satirday aboute Michellmas day,[8] was xij monethes, in the house of the said John Browne, then and ther [he] said that the sacrament of the aulter was but oonly brede and not Crists bodye: no moo beyng present, as he saith, but the said John Browne and this deponent. And he saith that he never comyned with the said John nor never herde hym comyn at any other tyme.

Examyned further [he] saith that the said John Browne of Assheford

---

6 25 March, feast of the Annunciation.
7 19 May, feast of St. Dunstan.
8 Michaelmas was kept on 29 September.

came to the house of this deponent in Rowenden, where and whan the said John Browne, this deponent and Johane his wif – and no moo persones then beyng present – in an evenyng sittyng by the fyre, in the hall of this deponent, had communicacion ayenst the sacrament of the aulter. And then and there they three togider concluded, affermed, held and beleved that the sacrament of the aulter was not the body of Criste, flesshe and bloode, but oonly brede. And then and there this deponent in the presence of the said John Browne charged and commaunded his said wif that she shuld not utter nor disclose their said communicacion upon payne of hir lif.

Also this deponent saith that aboute Shroftyde,[9] was ii or iii yeres passed, this deponent and Johane his wif and the saide John Browne, sittyng all togider by the fyre etyng and drynkyng, had communicacion ayenst worshipping of images of seynts and goyng on pilgremages. And then and there the said John Browne, this deponent and Johane his wif concluded, helde, beleved and affermed and everyche of theym held, concluded and affermed that the money that was offred to the images was but spent in waste.

Deposition of Philip Harwode. Philippe Harwode de Rowenden, xxix yeres of age, sworn and examyned, saith that John Browne, cutler, of Assheford upon seynt Annes daye,[10] was xii moneths, betwene the house of the said John Browne and the parisshe churche of Assheford commyned with the said Philippe ayenst the sacrament of the aulter, saying that the sacrament of the aulter was not God but oonly brede: and also that worshipping of images in the churche was not to be doon, for they were made with mannys hands and the seynts were in heven. And, as he remembreth, he hadde never more communicacion with the said John Browne nor the said John Browne with hym, but oonly that oon tyme. Moreover he saith that the said John Browne bade hym that he shuld kepe councaill of the said communicacion, for and if it were knowen they shuld be undoon thereby. And he saith that there was no man present but they.

His previous abjuration. Deinde xij[mo] die mensis Maii anno Domini et loco immediate predictis, coram prefato reverendissimo patre iudicialiter pro tribunali sedente, assidente eidem reverendo patre Roffense episcopo,[11] presentibus tunc ibidem etiam venerabilibus magistris Cuthberto Tunstall, utriusque iuris, Gabrieli Silvester, Clemente Browne et Petro Potkyn, legum doctoribus, et aliis, comparuit personaliter prefatus Johannes Browne. Cui idem reverendissimus pater ministravit articulos subsequentes videlicet.

---

[9] Shrove Tuesday fell on 20 February in 1509, 7 March in 1508.
[10] 26 July, feast of St. Anne.
[11] John Fisher, Bishop of Rochester, 1504–35.

Tibi, Johanni Browne, obiicimus et articulamur quod tu olim coram reverendissimo patre et domino, domino Johanne[12] cardinali Cantuariense archiepiscopo, omnem heresim contra fidem catholicam et ecclesiam apostolicam et sancte matris ecclesie dogmata – pro eo et ex eo quod tunc coram eodem certos articulos contra doctrinam sancte matris ecclesie sapientes et expresse per eandem sanctam ecclesiam reprobatos tenuisti et affirmasti et credidisti – in presencia dicti reverendissimi patris cardinalis expresse et in scriptis publice et solemniter abiurasti. Quibus articulis idem Johannes respondit prout sequitur in vulgari videlicet.

The said John, examyned upon the articules abovesaid, saith that he was abjured bifore my lord Morton, cardinal and archebisshop of Caunterbury, at Maidston aboute seynt Bartholomew tyde,[13] was xii yeres paste, for holding ayenst the sacrament of the aulter and confession and goyng to pylgremages. And he bare a fagot for his penaunce. And the same errors he lernyd of oon John Riche, whiche was burned, as he thynketh, att Halden in the diocise of Canterbury. And he saith that he dide abjure the said errors the tyme and place abovesaid.

Presentation of the depositions. Preterea tunc ibidem in presencia dicti Johannis Browne idem reverendissimus pater perlegi fecit dicta testium superius nominatorum contra dictum Johannem, ut prefertur, productorum et huiusmodi dicta et depositiones publicavit. Quibus dictis et depositionibus sic publicatis et perlectis, ipsisque testibus huiusmodi sua dicta et depositiones facie ad faciem coram ipso Johanne affirmantibus, dominus assignavit eidem Johanni Browne diem Mercurii proxime futurum ad dicendum, allegandum et excipiendum quod faciat pro eius defensione legitima in hac parte.

His reply, and declaration of the sentence. Item xix° die mensis Maii anno Domini et loco quibus supra, coram eodem reverendissimo patre tunc ibidem iudicialiter sedente, assidente eidem reverendo patre et domino, domino Ricardo Norwicense episcopo,[14] presentibus tunc ibidem venerabilibus viris magistris Cuthberto Tunstall, utriusque iuris, Roberto Wodward, legum, Gabrieli Silvestre, sacre pagine, doctoribus, et Johanne Esterfeld[15] ac aliis, comparuit personaliter dictus Johannes Browne. Quem idem reverendissimus pater interrogavit si quid haberet proponendum aut allegandum quod faciat ad sui defensionem. Qui quidem Johannes nichil allegavit aut proposuit in ea parte. Unde idem reverendissimus pater tunc ibidem tulit sentenciam contra eundem in

---

12 John Morton, Archbishop of Canterbury 1486–1500 and a cardinal from 1493.
13 See above, 22, note 1.
14 Richard Nykke, Bishop of Norwich, 1501–35.
15 See *BRUO*, i, 649, John Esterfeld.

scriptis. Per quam ipsum Johannem pro heretico relapso et incorrigibili condempnavit et manu seculari relinquendum decrevit. Cuius sentencie tenor sequitur et est talis.

Sentence. In Dei nomine, Amen. Nos,[u] [fo. 174r] Willelmus[v] permissione divina Cantuariensis archiepiscopus, totius Anglie primas et apostolice sedis legatus, in quodam negocio heretice pravitatis et relapsus in eandem contra te, Johannem Browne de Assherford nostre Cantuariensis diocesis laicum ac nostre iurisdictioni notorie subditum et subiectum, coram nobis in iudicio personaliter comparentem, ex officio nostro mero, rite et canonice procedentes – auditis et intellectis, visis, cognitis rimatisque ac matura deliberatione discussis et ponderatis dicti negocii meritis, servatisque in omnibus et per omnia in eodem negocio de iure servandis et quomodolibet requisitis – pro tribunali sedentes et solum Deum pre oculis nostris habentes.

Quia per acta, actitata, deducta et probata coram nobis in negocio antedicto, ac per te confessata, recognita et exhibita etiam coram nobis in eodem, invenimus te – postquam nonnullos hereses, errores et damnatas opiniones iuri divino et ecclesiastico, fidei catholice ac determinationi sancte matris ecclesie obviantes, repugnantes et contrarias coram recondende memorie domino Johanne Morton, miseratione divina tituli sancte Anastasie sacrosancte Romane ecclesie persbitero cardinali, Cantuariense archiepiscopo predecessore nostro, iudice in ea parte competente in iudicio, in forma ecclesie consueta manifeste et solemniter abiurasti – in eosdem hereses, errores et damnatas opiniones huiusmodi reincidisse et recidinasse ac eos et eas tam in nostra diocesi Cantuariense antedicta quam alibi in dicta nostra provincia Cantuariense animo deliberato asseruisse, tenuisti, credidisse, affirmasse et docuisse: te, Johannem Browne predictum, de consilio iurisperitorum hic presentium et nobis assidentium et assistentium, in hereses et errores predictos alias per te, ut promittitur, abiuratos fuisse et esse manifeste recidivum et relapsum pronunciamus, decernimus et declaramus per hanc nostram sententiam diffinitivam, quam ferimus in hiis scriptis: teque, eundem Johannem Browne, curie sive iudicio seculari ad omnem iuris effectum qui exinde sequi debeat aut poterit relinquendum fore decernimus, et sic relinquimus per presentes.

Relinquishing of him to the secular arm. Excellentissimo principi etc., ut supra.[16] Datum in manerio nostro de Knoll xixº Maii anno Domini mº ccccmº xiº et nostre translationis anno viiiº.

---

[16] See above, 25.

---

[u] Willelmus *at foot of page.*   [v] Sententia contra Browne *in margin.*

7. PROCEEDINGS AGAINST EDWARD WALKER OF MAIDSTONE, 8 MAY TO
3 OCTOBER, 1511 [fos. 174R–175R]

His appearance in court. Octavo die mensis Maii anno Domini
millesimo quingentesimo undecimo in capella manerii reverendissimi
patris et domini, domini Willelmi permissione divina Cantuariensis
archiepiscopi, totius Anglie primatis et apostolice sedis legati, de
Lamehith, coram eodem reverendissimo patre pro tribunali iudicialiter
sedente, presentibus et assidentibus eidem venerabilibus viris magistris
Johanne Colet, sacre theologie professore, decano ecclesie cathedralis
sancti Pauli Londoniensis, Thoma Wodyngton, decretorum doctore,
curie Cantuariensis officiali, Cuthberto Tunstall, utriusque iuris
doctore, Thoma Perte, legum, Gabrieli Silvestre, sacre pagine,
doctoribus, et pluribus aliis, comparuit personaliter Edwardus Walker
de Maidston, cutler, Cantuariensis diocesis. Quem idem reverendissimus pater iurare fecit ad sancta Dei evangelia de fideliter
respondendo certis articulis contra eum in negocio heretice pravitatis ex
officio dicti reverendissimi patris ministratis. Quorum articulorum
tenores sequuntur videlicet.

Charges against him. In[a] Dei nomine, Amen. Nos, Willelmus
permissione divina Cantuariensis archiepiscopus, totius Anglie primas
et apostolice sedis legatus, tibi, Edwardo Walker de Maidston nostre
Cantuariensis diocesis ac nostre iurisdictioni notorie subdito et
subiecto, ad meram anime tue correctionem necnon ad omne iuris
effectum qui exinde sequi poterit aut debebit, obiicimus et articulamur
coniunctim et divisim omnes et singulos articulos infrascriptos et
quamlibet partem et particulam eorundem: mandantes et precipientes
quatinus eisdem omnibus et singulis singulariterque in eisdem[b]
contentis plenam, meram et nudam respondeas veritatem sub pena iuris.
    In[c] primis tibi obiicimus et articulamur quod tu fuisti et es nostre
Cantuariensis diocesis ac nostre iurisdictioni notorie subditus et
subiectus.
    Item[d] quod tu per plures annos elapsos omnes et singulos hereses,
errores et damnatas opiniones subsequentes seu saltem aliquos
credidisti, docuisti, tenuisti, affirmasti et predicasti, videlicet.
    Quod in sacramento altaris sive eucharistie non est verum corpus
Christi sed panis materialis.
    Item[e] quod sacramenta baptismi et confirmationis non sunt
necessaria ad salutem anime.

---

[a] Edwardus Walker *in margin.*   [b] *MS.* eidem.   [c] i *in margin.*   [d] ii *in margin.*
[e] iii *in margin.*

Item^f quod vocalis,^g auricularis sive verbalis confessio peccatorum non est facienda sacerdoti.

Item^h quod nulla potestas fuit aut est sacerdotibus a Deo collata magis quam laicis in sacramentis ecclesie ministrandis, missis celebrandis aut aliis divinis officiis exequendis.

Item^i quod matrimonii solennisatio non est necessaria ad anime salutem nec a iure divino instituta.

Item^j quod sacramentum extreme unctionis non est utile aut necessarium ad anime salutem.

Item^k quod imagines sancte crucis et crucifixi ac beate Marie virginis et aliorum sanctorum nullo modo sunt venerande, sed quod venerantes huiusmodi imagines committunt idolatriam.

Item^l quod peregrinationes ad loca sancta et devota, ubi solet populus christianus sanctos et reliquias sanctorum venerari, non sunt necessarie sive meritorie ad salutem anime sed damnabiles, detestando huiusmodi peregrinaciones et peregrinantes ad huiusmodi loca reprehendendo, dicendo huiusmodi peregrinantes sic peregrinando committere idolatriam.

Item^m quod orationes non sunt effundende ad sanctos sed ad solum Deum, qui solus audit orantes.

Item^n quod panis benedictus et aqua benedicta non sunt maioris virtutis et efficacie post benedictionem factam a sacerdote quam ante benedictionem.

Item^o quod tu omnes et singulos hereses, errores et damnatas opiniones supradictos seu eorum aliquos credis, doces, tenes, affirmas et predicas etiam in presenti.

Item^p quod tu omnia et singula premissa timore probationum solum et ad evadendam penam es confessus. Et si detecta per alios non fuissent nec timeres te posse convinci per testes, casu quo illa negares premissa nunquam sponte confessus fuisses. Nec ea nunc sponte sed timore probationum confiteris.

Item^q quod tu cum aliis personis de prefatis heresibus, erroribus et damnatis opinionibus secum communicantibus sepius et iteratis vicibus communicasti: et ut quod habuisti et habes libros concernentes dictos errores.

His reply to the charges. Qui quidem Edwardus Walker, tunc ibidem examinatus et interrogatus de et super articulis huiusmodi, fatetur se fuisse et esse iurisdictionis dicti reverendissimi patris. Reliquos articulos omnes et singulos publice tunc ibidem negavit.

---

^f iiii *in margin.*   ^g vocalis *repeated.*   ^h v *in margin.*   ^i vi *in margin.*
^j vii *in margin.*   ^k viii *in margin.*   ^l ix *in margin.*   ^m x *in margin.*
^n xi *in margin.*   ^o xii *in margin.*   ^p xiii *in margin.*   ^q xiiii *in margin.*

The witnesses. Et deinde tunc ibidem prefatus reverendissimus pater produci fecit in testes contra dictum Edwardum Walker, ad convincendum eundem, Stephanum Castelyn de Tenterden, cutler, Willelmum Baker de Crainebroke, Robertum Reynold de Benynden, Johannem Bampton de Brasted,ʳ Robertum Bright de Maidston et Willelmum Ryche de Benynden. [Et eosdem,] in presencia dicti Edwardi Walker, ad sancta Dei evangelia iurare fecit de dicendo veritatem quam noverint de opinione dicti Edwardi contra catholicam fidem et ecclesie universalis determinationem. Quorum dicta et depositiones sequuntur videlicet.

Deposition of Stephen Castelyn. Stephyn Castelyn de Tenterden, cutler, of the age of xxiii yeres, sworne and examyned upon the opinions of Edward Walker ayenst the sacraments of the churche, saith that aboute Shroftetyde,[1] was xii moneths, in the house of the said Edward Walker at Maidston, in the kechyn by the fyre on the evenyng, the said Edward Walker, Robert Hylles and this deponent commyned togider ayenst the sacrament of the aulter. And then and ther they three and every of theym concluded and said that the sacrament of the aulter was but oonly brede, doon in a mynde to call people togider, and God was oonly in heven. And also, as he remembreth, they commyned agaynst pilgremages.

Deposition of William Baker. William Baker of Crainebroke, wittnes sworne and examyned upon the opinions of Edward Walker ayenst the sacraments of the churche etc., saith that on Maye day,[2] was xii yeres, this deponent, Stephyn Castelyn and Robert Reynold were togider with Edwarde Walker in the same Edwards house in Maidston. When and where this deponent, Edward Walker, Stephyn Castelyn and Robert Reynold and everyche of them commyned, held, concluded and beleved that the sacrament of the aulter, that the preest dude holde above his hede at the sacryng tyme, was not Crists body, flesshe and bloode, but oonly brede.

Item this deponent saith [fo. 174v] that at Cristmas, was xii monethes, upon Childermas[3] nyght this deponent, John Bampton, William Ryche and another yong man of Bamptons acquayntaunce came togider to the house of Edward Walker of Maideston. At whiche tyme the said William Baker, John Bampton, William Riche and the said yong man of Bamptons acquayntaunce and everyche of theym

[1] Shrove Tuesday fell on 12 February in 1510.
[2] 1 May.
[3] Childermas, 28 December, the feast of the Holy Innocents.

ʳ Brasted *sic,* possibly a scribal error for Bearsted.

commyned, held, concluded and beleved that the sacrament of the aulter, that the preest did hold above his hede at the sacrying tyme, was not Crists body, fleshe and bloode, but oonly brede. Also this deponent saith that he dide redde unto John Bampton, William Riche, Edward Walker and to the same yong man, Walkers[s] acquayntaunce, upon the said Childermas nyght in the house of the said Walker a booke of Mathewe, whereyn was conteyned the gospell in Englisshe. With the whiche redyng the said John Bampton, William Riche, Edward Walker and the said yong man were wele contentid and pleasid, saying that it was pitie that it might not be knowen openly. The whiche redyng in the said booke, as they understood it, was ayenst the sacraments of the aulter, baptisme, matrymony and preesthode. Examyned where the said booke is become, he saith that John Bampton receyved it of hym, and where the said Bampton hath bestowed it he cannot tell.

Also this deponent saith that on May daye bifore rehersed, in the said house of Edward Walkers, this deponent, Edward Walker, Stephyn Castelyn and Robert Reynold and every of theym had communicacion ayenst pilgremages and worshipping of seynts and of offeryngs. And then and there they and every of theym concluded that it shuld not be profitable for mannys soule. In so moche that aftir the said communicacion this deponent, whiche was mynded to goo and offer to the roode of grace, owtdrewe his mynde and went not thider but gave his offeryng to a poore man.

Deposition of Robert Reynold. Robert Reynold, sworn and examyned upon the opinions of Edward Walker ayenst the sacraments of holy churche, saith that on May daye, was ii yeres, this deponent, Stephyn Castelyn, William Baker and Edward Walker of Maideston, in the house of the said Walker, commyned togider ayenst the sacrament of the aulter. And then and ther they concluded, beleved, held and defendid and so every of theym held, concluded, beleved and defended that the sacrament of the aulter was not Crists body, flesshe and bloode, but a thing made in mynde and for the remembraunce of Criste for the people, for Crists owne body was in heven and his worde was in erthe.

Also this deponent saith yat aboute seynt Barthilmew tyde,[4] was xii monethes, in the house of the said Walker, this deponent, the said Edward Walker, John Bampton and Stephyn Castelyn had communicacion togider ayenst the sacrament of the aulter. Than and there all they togider, as this deponent now remembreth, concluded that the sacrament of the aulter was but materiall brede and not the body of Criste.

---

[4] See above, 22, note 1.

[s] *Sic.*

Deposition of John Bampton. John Bampton of Barsted, xxxiii yeres of age, sworn and examyned upon the opinions of Edward Walker ayenst the sacraments of the churche, saith that aboute Cristmas, was xii monethes, in an evenyng in the house of Edward Walker of Maideston, William Baker or Stephen Castelyn dide rede in a booke to this deponent, William Riche and Edward Walker, and as he remembreth Thomas Feld then beyng present there, and taught ayenst the sacrament of the aulter, saying that it was but brede made by man and not Crists body, flesshe and bloode. To the whiche teching all they, that is to say this deponent, William Baker, William Riche and Edward Walker, gave credence, faith and assent without contradiccion. And as touching Thomas Feld, he nowe remembreth not wheder he were there present or no, but as he thynketh he was there and dide holde like opinions as all they dide att that same tyme.

Deposition of Robert Bright. Robert Bright of Maideston of the age of lx yeres, cordynar, sworn and examyned the xxiiii[th] day of May the yere of our Lord mille v[c]xi, saith that he hath dwell in Maideston these ii yeres last passed, and ii yeres next bifore that he dwellid at Berghstede, and was borne at Berfold beside Ippiswiche,[5] from whens he departid more then xx yeres past.

Examyned upon the first article concernyng the sacrament of the aulter, he saith that he hath beleved that the sacrament of the aulter was not Crists very body, flesshe and bloode, but oonly brede. Examyned how long tyme he hath soo beleved and by whom he was first induced so to beleve, he aunswereth and saith that aboute midsomer last past as he can remember, beyng in the house of John Bampton of Berghstede, the same John Bampton said and taught this deponent that the sacrament of the aulter was not the body of God, flesshe and bloode, as preests said it was, but it was oonly brede and geven from God. For Crist hymself in his owne body gave brede to his disciples and not his owne body, and so doo preests in lykewise geve brede that cometh from God in remebraunce of the brede geven by Criste in his maundy. According to the whiche teching this deponent saith that he dide beleve that the sacrament of the aulter was not Crists body but oonly brede. And that aftir that tyme divers and sondry other tymes this deponent comyned with the said John Bampton in the same Johns house, holding and affermyng that the sacrament of the aulter was not Crists body.

And he saith that there were present togider in the said John Bamptons house at aftir none on mydsomer day last past, the said John Bampton, his brother Richard Bampton of Boxley, Thomas Feld and

5 Bergholt(?), near Ipswich.

this deponent. And at Cristmas last past were present in the same house of John Bampton the said John Bampton, Richard Bampton, Thomas Feld, William Baker of Crainebroke, Stephen Castelyn, William Riche and this deponent. At the whiche bothe tymes all the forsaid named persones and every of theym commyned, held, beleved and affermed that the sacrament of the aulter was not the body of Criste but oonly brede. Item he saith that at Cristmas aforsaid there was also a yong persone of a xvii yere of age yn the company and communicacion aforsaid, whiche yong man came with William Riche, as this deponent remembreth, but he knoweth not his name.

Also this deponent saith that at Cristmas aforsaid in the nyght tyme all the said persones togider went from John Bamptons house to the house of Edward Walker of Maidston and there all they togider with the said Edward Walker and . . . ᵗ the wife of the same Walker commyned, herd, assentid and affermed without contradiccion ayenst the blissed sacrament of the aulter, that it was nott Crists verey body, fleshe and bloode, but oonly brede. And as they were so commynyng . . . ᵘ the wif of yat said Walker said, 'Sires, it is not good that ye talke moche here of thies maters for the jaylors will take hede of you yf ye come huder. And also beware for som folks will comyn hider anon.' And therupon furthwith came yn the jaylors wif and they cessed of their communicacion.

Deposition of William Riche. William Riche of Benynden of the age of xl yeres, sworn the vᵗʰ dayᵛ of Maye anno Domini mille vᶜ xi, saith that on seynt Stephen day⁶ at nyght, was xii monethes, came unto hes house William Baker of Crainebroke and John Bampton of Othan, whiche lay at this deponents house all that nyght. And on seynt Johns day⁷ next folowing they thre went to Othan at John Bamptons house. At all the which places and tymes they iii togider and every of theym, and also a yong man that came with Bampton, [fo. 175r] commyned ayenst the sacrament of the aulter and held and maynteyned that the sacrament of the aulter was not Crists body but oonly brede.

He saith also that from John Bamptons house they went to Walkers house in Maideston in the nyght. Where and when the said John Baker, John Bampton, William Riche and Edward satt drynkyng and began to comyne of their matiers furthwieth they came thidder, that is to say ayenst the sacrament of the aulter. And held and beleved they iiii all togiders that it was not Godds body but brede oonly. How be it, he saith, their talkyng was not long bicause the jaylors wife and another

---

⁶ 26 December, feast of St. Stephen.
⁷ 27 December, feast of St. John the Evangelist.

ᵗ *Blank space in MS.*   ᵘ *Blank space in MS.*   ᵛ vᵗʰ day *sic.*

woman came into the house where they sate talking. And therfore Edward Walker, beyng aferde to be suspected and espied, spake to that other iii saying, 'Sirs, drynke ye and make ye mery and high you from hens agayn!' And so they departid agayn.

Presentation of the depositions. Item decimo die mensis Maii predicti, anno et loco quibus supra, coram dicto reverendissimo patre tunc ibidem pro tribunali iudicialiter sedente, assidente eidem reverendissimo patre Roffense episcopo, presentibus tunc ibidem venerabilibus viris magistris Cuthberto Tunstall, Gabrieli Silvestre, Clemente Browne, Thoma Perte, Petro Potkyn, doctoribus, et pluribus aliis, comparuit personaliter prefatus Edwardus Walker. In cuius presencia idem reverendissimus pater publicavit dicta testium predictorum, et huiusmodi dicta et depositiones tunc ibidem publice perlegi fecit. Et assignavit eidem Edwardo diem Lune proxime futurum ad allegandum, proponendum et excipiendum quod faciat pro sua legitima defensione quare pro heretico convicto declarari non debeat.

His reply. Quo die adveniente, videlicet duodecimo die mensis Maii predicti, anno et loco quibus supra, coram eodem reverendissimo patre iudicialiter pro tribunali sedente, presentibus personis superius nominatis, comparuit personaliter Edwardus Walker predictus, habens hos diem et locum ad proponendum, allegandum et excipiendum contra testes et eorum dicta quod faciat pro sua defensione legitima. Quem idem reverendissimus pater interrogavit tunc ibidem si quid haberet sic allegandum et proponendum. Qui respondit huiusmodi testes falso deposuisse contra eum et se non novisse aliquem eorum preter Stephanum Castlyn. Deinde testibus huiusmodi ibidem adductis coram eo, et deposicionibus tunc ibidem publice iterum in presencia dicti Edwardi perlectis, testibus antedictis huiusmodi sua dicta et depositiones facie ad faciem contra ipsum Edwardum affirmantibus, ipse tamen Edwardus constanter negavit ut prius.

His later reply, and declaration of the sentence. Insuper tercio die mensis Septembris anno Domini predicto in capella dicti reverendissimi patris de Maideston, presentibus tunc ibidem coram eodem reverendissimo patre, assidentibus eidem, reverendo patre Cironenense episcopo et domino . . . ᵂ priore de Ledys,[8] presentibusque venerabilibus viris magistris Cuthberto Tunstall, Gabrieli Silvestre, superius nominatis, et

---

[8] Prior of the Augustinian canons at Leeds, Kent.

ᵂ *Blank space in MS.*

magistro Thoma Millyng,[9] in utroque iure bacallario, ac pluribus aliis, comparuit personaliter dictus Edwardus Walker. Et tunc ibidem negavit, ut prius, singula contra eum obiecta. Unde prefatus reverendissimus pater, iudicialiter pro tribunali ut prefertur sedens, tulit sentenciam contra eundem in scriptis. Per quam ipsum hereticum impenitentem et incorrigilibem pronunciavit et declaravit ac manui seculari relinquendum fore decrevit. Cuius sentencie tenor sequitur et est talis.

Sentence. In[x] Dei nomine, Amen. Nos, Willelmus permissione divina Cantuariensis archiepiscopus, totius Anglie primas et apostolice sedis legatus, in quodam negocio heretice pravitatis contra te, Edwardum Walker nostre Cantuariensis diocesis ac nostre iurisdictioni subditum et subiectum, coram nobis in iudicio personaliter comparentem, nobis super heretica pravitate huiusmodi detectum et delatum ac per nostram diocesim Cantuariensem antedictam notorie et publice in ea parte apud bonos et graves diffamatum, ex officio nostro mero, rite et canonice procedentes – auditis et intellectis, visis, cognitis rimatisque ac matura deliberacione discussis et ponderatis dicti negocii meritis, servatisque in omnibus et per omnia in eodem negocio de iure servandis ac quomodolibet requisitis – pro tribunali sedentes, Christi nomine invocato, et solum Deum pre oculis habentes.

Quia per acta, actitata, deducta, probata et exhibita coram nobis in eodem negocio invenimus te per probationes legitimas coram nobis in hac parte iudicialiter factas nonnullos et varios errores, hereses et damnatas opiniones iuri divino et ecclesiastico obviantes, contrarios et repugnantes contra fidem orthodoxam per universalem, catholicam et apostolicam ecclesiam determinatam et observatam tenuisse, credidisse, affirmasse, predicasse et dogmatisasse et presertim contra sacramentum altaris seu eucharistie et alia sacramenta et sancte matris ecclesie dogmata. Et quamvis nos, Christi vestigiis inherendo, qui non vult mortem peccatoris sed magis ut convertatur et vivat, sepe numero conati fuimus te corrigere ac viis et modis licitis et canonicis, quibus potuimus aut scivimus, ad fidem orthodoxam per univesalem, catholicam et apostolicam ecclesiam determinatam et observatam ac ad unitatem sancte matris ecclesie reducere. Tamen invenimus te adeo dure cervicis quod tuos errores et hereses huiusmodi nolueris sponte et incontinente confiteri, nec ad fidem catholicam et unitatem sancte matris ecclesie antedictas debite reverti et redire. Sed tanquam iniquitatis et tenebrarum filius in tantum indurasti cor tuum ut non velis intelligere vocem tui pastoris tibi paterno compatientis affectu. Nec

[9] See *BRUO*, ii, 1333, Thomas Myllyng.

velis piis et paternis monitionibus allici nec salubribus reduci
blandiciis.

Nos vero, nolentes quod tu qui nequam es fias nequior, et gregem
dominicum in futurum tua heretice pravitatis labe de quo plurimum
timemus inficias, idcirco, de iurisperitorum consilio nobis in hac parte
assistentium cum quibus communicavimus in hac parte, te, Edwardum
Walker predictum, demeritis atque culpis per tuam damnabilem
pertinaciam aggravatis, de et [super] huiusmodi detestabili heretice
pravitatis reatu convictum et ad ecclesie unitatem penitencialiter redire
nolentem, hereticum hereticisque credentem ac eorum fautorem et
receptatorem pretextu premissorum fuisse et esse cum dolore et
amaritudine cordis indicamus et declaramus sentencialiter et diffinitive
in his scriptis: relinquentes te ex nunc tanquam hereticum iudicio sive
curie seculari. Teque, Edwardum predictum ut prefertur, hereticum
nichilominus in maioris excommunicationis sententiam occasione
premissorum incidisse et incurrisse necnon excommunicatum fuisse et
esse pronunciamus, decernimus et declaramus etiam in hiis scriptis.

Relinquishing of him to the secular arm. Excellentissimo principi et
domino, domino Henrico Dei gratia regi Anglie et Francie et domino
Hibernie illustrissimo, Willelmus permissione divina Cantuariensis
archiepiscopus, totius Anglie primas et apostolice sedis legatus:
salutem in eo per quem reges regnant et principes dominantur.

Vestre regie celsitudini tenore presencium significamus quod quidam
iniquitatis filius Edwardus Walker, propter suos varios damnatos et
manifestos errores et hereses necnon opiniones damnabiles contra
fidem catholicam et sanctam matrem ecclesiam per eundem nonnullis
modis et mediis doctos et predicatos, per nos legitime et canonice
convictus est et hereticus iudicatus. Cum igitur sancta mater ecclesia
non habeat quod ulterius facere debeat in hac parte, vestre regie
celsitudini et brachio vestro seculari dictum hereticum relinquimus.

Datum in manerio nostro de Knoll tercio die mensis Octobris anno
Domini millesimo quingentesimo undecimo, et nostre translationis
anno octavo.

8. ABJURATION OF SIMON PIERS OF WALDERSHARE, 12 MAY, 1511
[fo. 175R–V]

His abjuration. In^a the name of God, Amen. Bifore you, maister Robert Wodeward, commissary unto the moost reverend fadir in God my lord William archbisshop of Canterbury, primate of all Englond, I, Symon Piers of the parisshe of Waldershare in the diocise of Caunterbury, of my pure harte and free will confesse and knowlege that in tymes past I have bylevid, saide, holden, affermed and taught of the articles of the faithe and of the doctrine of the churche otherwise then the holy churche of Rome and universall churche of God techeth, holdeth and observeth. And certayn open, dampnable errors and heresies countrary to the true catholike faithe and determinacion of holy churche I have bothe openly and secretly holden, bileved, affermed and taught. And specially amongest other, thies errours folowing, that is to wite.

That almighty God our lorde Jhesu Crist, very God eternal withoute begynnyng and very man incarnate, taking flesshe and bloode of the moost pure and glorious virgyn our lady seynt Mary, was [fo. 175v] God and man incarnate at the begynnyng of the worlde and before he was conceyved and borne of his said blissed moder and virgyn Mary.

Wherfore I, the said Simon, willing hereafter to belive in the faith of Crist and of his churche and to folowe the true doctrine of the same, with a pure hart forsake^b and utterly despise my said errour and damnable opinion and confesse it to be contrary to the faith of Crists holy churche and determinacion of the same. And therfore the saide error, heresie and opinion in especiall and all other errors, heresies, false doctrines and damned opinions contrary to the faith of Crist and of the churche aforsaid I in lykewise abjure, forsake and utterly renownce here bifore you and all the honorable audience here assembled. And over that I swere by thies holy evangelies by me bodily here touched that from hensforth I shall never holde, teche nor afferme the forsaid error, heresy and damnable opinion nor any other ayenst the faithe of Cristes holy churche and determynacion of the same, nor yet shall by myself or any other persone pryvatly or apertly defende, maynteyn, socour, favor or supporte any person that to my knowlege holdeth, bileveth, affermeth or techeth any suche errours, heresies or damnable opinions or any persone that is suspected of the same. And if I may knowe hereaftir any persone giltye or suspect of suche errors, heresies or suche false and damnable opinions or any persone holding or keping any prevy companyes, assemblez or false doctrynes or any opinions contary to the commen doctryne of the churche aforsaid, or if

---

^a Abiuratio Simonis Piers *in margin.*   ^b *MS.* forsaid.

I may knowe of their fautors, comforters, concelours or defensours or any that have suspect books, quoyers or other writtings of any suche errors, heresies or damnable opinions, I shall withoute delaye geve knowlege unto my said lorde archebisshop of Caunterbury or unto the ordinary or ordinaries of the same persones or els unto his or their successours and officers. So God me helpe and holy dome and by thies holy evaungelies.

In wittnes wherof to thies presents I have with myn owne hande made a signe of the holy crosse +

Note. Facta fuit premissa abiuratio per prefatum Simonem Piers et per eundem perlecta in forma predicta xii° die mensis Maii anno Domini millesimo quingentesimo undecimo in ecclesia cathedrali Christi Cantuariense coram commissario prefato: presentibus tunc et ibidem magistris Roberto Goseburne,[1] in artibus magistro, Johanne Williamson, in decretis bacallario, et Rogero Downevilde,[2] in legibus baccallario, Johanne Colman[3] et Thoma Laurence, notariis publicis, scribis in hac parte assumptis, et aliis quamplurimis testibus.

[1] See *BRUO*, ii, 793–4, Robert Gosebourne.
[2] See *BRUO*, i, 584–5, Roger Domvile.
[3] See Woodcock, *Canterbury*, 39 and 120.

9. ABJURATIONS AND PENANCES OF THOMAS, JOAN AND PHILIP HARWODE
OF ROLVENDEN, JOHN BAMPTON OF BOXLEY AND STEPHEN CASTELYN OF
TENTERDEN, 15 MAY, 1511 [fos. 161V–162R]

Their appearance in court etc. Quintodecimo die mensis Maii anno
Domini supradicto in capella manerii dicti reverendissimi patris de
Lamehith, presentibus tunc ibidem magistris Cuthberto Tunstall,
eiusdem reverendissimi patris cancellario, Roberto Wodwarde,
commissario eiusdem reverendissimi patris, Gabriele Silvester, sacre
theologie professore, Johanne Estfeld et notariis superius nominatis[1] ac
aliis, coram eodem reverendissimo patre iudicialiter sedente, comparuerunt personaliter Thomas Harwode de Rollynden Cantuariensis
diocesis, Johanna Harwode uxor eiusdem, et Philippus Harwode filius
eorundem, Johannes Bampton de Boxley ac Stephanus Castelyn de
Tenderden. Ac omnem heresim et erroneas[a] opiniones contra fidem
catholicam et ecclesie universalis determinacionem quas ibidem se
tenuisse confessi sunt, publice abiurarunt in forma qua supradicti
abiurantes[2] abiurarunt, iuxta contenta in scedulis suarum abiurationum
per eos et eorum quemlibet tunc ibidem publice recitatis et manibus
suis propriis signo crucis signatis: prestito primitus per eosdem, ad
sancta Dei evangelia per eorum singulos corporaliter tacta, de
perimplendo penitentiam eis in hac parte iniungendam iuramento
corporali. Quarum scedularum tenores sequuntur videlicet.

Abjuration of Thomas, Joan and Philip Harwode. In[b] the name of God,
Amen. Bifore you, the moost reverend fader in God my lorde
archebisshop of Caunterbury, we, Thomas Harwode, Johane Harwode
and Philipp Harwode of Rowenden of yor diocise of Canterbury, of
my[c] pure hert and free will confesse and knowlege that we in tymes
passed bifore this houre, that is to witte by the space of three yeres and
more, have beleved, thought, said, holden, affirmed and taught of the
sacraments of the churche and of the articles of the faith otherwise then
the holy church of Rome and universall churche of God techeth,
holdeth and observeth. And many and divers open and damned errors
and heresies contrarie to the true and catholik faith and determinacion
of holy church we have bothe secretly and openly holden, beleved,
affirmed and taught. And specially among other, these errors and
heresies folowing, that is to wite.

---

[1] Thomas Laurence, William Potkyn and David Cooper (see above, 26).
[2] That is, the ten abjurors recorded in section 5 (above, 26–42).

---

[a] *MS.* erroneos.   [b] Thomas Harwod, Johanna Harwod, Philippus Harwod *in margin.*
[c] *Sic, first person singular here and elsewhere in this abjuration.*

First, that the sacrament of the aulter ys not Crists verey body but materiall brede.

Also that confession of synnes aught not to be made to a preest, and that confession is not profitable for a mannys soule that is made to a prest, for it shuld be made oonly to God in mynde.

Also that pilgremages to holy and devoute places be not necessary nother meritorious for mannys soule.

Also that ymages of the crucifixe, of our Lady and of holy seynts be not to be worshipped.

Wherfore we, the forsaid Thomas, Johane and Philippe, willing hereaftir to beleve in the feith of Criste and of his churche and to folowe the true doctryne of holy church, with a pure hert forsake and utterly despise my said errors, heresies and damnable opinions and confesse theym to be contrarious and repugnaunt to the faith of Criste and determinacion of his holy churche. And therfore the said errors, heresies and opinions in especiall and all other errors and heresies, fals doctrynes and damned opinions in generall likewise contrary and repugnaunt to the faith of Crist and determinacion of his church aforsaid we abjure, forsake and utterly renownce here bifore yor gracious lordship and all the honorable audience here assembled. And over that I swer by these holy evangelies by us bodely here touched that from hensforth we shall never hold, teche, beleve or afferme the forsaid errors, heresies and damnable opinions nor noon other ayenst the faith of Cristes holy churche and determinacion of the same. Nor yet we shall by ourself or any other persone pryvatly or apertly defende, maynten, favor, socour or support any persone that to our knowlege holdeth, beleveth, affermeth or techeth any suche error, heresie or damned opinion nor any persone that is suspect of the same. And if we may knowe hereafter any persone of suche error, heresie or of any suche fals doctrynes or any opinions contrary to the commen doctryne of the church aforsaid, or if we may knowe any of their fautors, comfortors, concelors or defensors or any yat have suspect books or quayers of suche errors, heresies and dampnable opinions, we shall without delaye geve knowlege unto yor good lordship or to yor successors or unto the ordinarye or ordinaries of the same persones or ells unto yor and their officers. So God me helpe and holy dome and thies holy evangelies.

In wittnes wherof to these presents with our owne hands we have made and subscribed the signe of the holy crosse. Thomas Harwod + Johane Harwod + Philipp Harwode +

Abjuration of Stephen Castelyn. In[d] the name of God, Amen. Bifore you, the most reverend fader in God my lord William archibisshop of

---

[d] Stephanus Castellyn *in margin.*

Caunterbury, I, Stephyn Castellyn of Tenterden of yor diocise of Caunterbury, of my pure hart and fre will confesse and knowlege that I in tymes passed bifore this houre, that is to witte by the space of iiii yeres and more, have bileved, thought, said, holden, affirmed and taught of the sacraments of the church and of the articles of the faith otherwise than the holy church of Rome and universall church of God holdeth, techeth and observeth. And many and diverse open and damned errors and heresies contrarie to the true and catholik faith and determinacion of holy church I have both secretely and openly holden, beleved, affermed and taught. And specially among other, these errors and heresies folowing, that is to wite.

First, that the sacrament of the aulter ys not Crists verey body but materiall brede.

Also that pilgremages to holy and devoute places be not necessary nother meriotrious for mannys soule.

Also that images of seynts be not to be worshipped.

Also that a prest was not sufficient to here a mannys confession and absoile hym of his synnes, for suche absolution of a prest was nothing profitable for a mannys soule, but that confession was to be made oonly to God by mynde.

Wherfore I, the said Stephen Castellyn, willing hereaftir to beleve in the faith of Criste and of his church and to folowe the true doctryne of the same, with a pure hert forsake and utterly despise my said errors, hereies and damnable opinions and confesse theym to be contrariouse and repugnaunt to the faith of Criste and determinacion of his holy church. And therfore the said errors, heresies and opinions in especiall and all other errors, heresies and damned opinions in generall [fo. 162r] likewise contrary and repugnaunt to the faith of Criste and determinacion of his church aforsaid I abjure, forsake and utterly renownce here bifore yor gracious lordship and all the honorable audience here assembled. And over that I swere by thies holy evangelies by me bodily here touched that from hensforth I shall never holde, teche, beleve or afferme the forsaid errores, heresies and damnable opinions nor noon other ayenst the faith of Crists holy church and determynacion of the same. Nor yet I shall by myself or any other persone privatly or apertly defende, maynten, socor, favor or support any persone that to my knowlege holdeth, beleveth, affermeth or techith any suche error, heresie or damned opinion nor any persone that is suspecte of the same. And if I may knowe hereaftir any persone of such errour, heresie or of any suche false doctrynes or any opinions contrary to the commyn doctryne of the churche aforsaid, or if I may knowe any of their fautors, comfortors, concelors and defensors or any that have suspecte books or quayers of suche errors, heresies and damnable opinions, I shall without delaye geve knowlege unto yor lordship or to yor successors or unto the ordinarye or ordinaries of the same persones or ells unto yor and theyre officers. Soo God me helpe and holy dome and thies holy evangelies.

In wittnes wherof to thies presents with myn owne hand I have made and subscribed my name [and] the signe of the holy crosse. Steven Castelyn +

Their penances. Quibus abiurationibus tunc ibidem factis, prefatus reverendissimus pater eisdem iniunxit videlicet, quod die Sabbati proximo ad octo dies apud Crainbroke, tempore quo publicum forum ibidem celebrabitur, gestabunt fasciculum ligneum super humerum trina vice circa forum, et abinde transeant ad ecclesiam cum eodem fasciculo et illud ibidem dimittant, et flexibus genibus ibidem dicent oracionem Dominicam, Ave Maria et Credo.

Item ulterius iniunxit eisdem Thome, Johanne, Philippo et Johanni quod duobus diebus Dominicis et festivis proximis post diem Sabbati ad octo dies eant, nudi pedes et tibias, cum fasciculis ligneis super humeris suis, more penitentium, ante processionem in ecclesiis suis parochialibus et stent per totum tempus misse cum eisdem fasciculis in medio ecclesie ibidem ante ostium chori.

Item quod non amoveant se a loco ubi iam inhabitant, nisi prius certificabunt eundem reverendissimum patrem seu eius successores de loco ubi manere intendunt.

Item quod revelabunt quoscumque noverint de heresi suspectos aut libros de heresi habentes.

Item quod frequentabunt suas ecclesias parochiales diebus Dominicis et festivis et ibidem divina audient ut boni Christiani.

Et insuper tunc ibidem reverendissimus pater iniunxit Stephano Castelyn quod gestabit fasciculum depictum, modo quo superius recitato,[3] super humero suo sinistro publice sine aliqua occultatione durante vita sua, nisi aliter fuerit secum dispensatum per eundem reverendissimum patrem aut suos successores sufficienter et legitime.

Item quod tribus Dominicis festivis, videlicet in die Dominica ad octo dies, gestabit fasciculum ligneum ante crucem in processione ecclesie sue parochialis, stando post processionem in medio ecclesie ante ostium chori usque ad finem misse.

Item quod non amovebit se a loco ubi iam inhabitat, nisi prius certificabit eundem reverendissimum patrem seu eius successores de loco ubi manere intendit.

Item quod revelabit dicto reverendissimo patri quos noverit suspectos aut libros de heresi habentes etc.

Item quod premissa perimplebit sub pena relapsus.

[3] See above, 40.

10. ABJURATIONS AND PENANCES OF WILLIAM BAKER OF CRANBROOK,
WILLIAM OLBERDE JUNIOR OF GODMERSHAM, ROBERT REIGNOLD OF
CRANBROOK AND THOMAS FELDE OF BOXLEY, 19 MAY, 1511 [fo. 162R–V]

Their appearance in court etc. Decimonono die mensis Maii predicti in
capella manerii de Lamehith predicti, coram eodem reverendissimo
patre pro tribunali iudicialiter sedente, assidente eidem reverendissimo
patre et domino, domino Ricardo Norwicense episcopo, presentibus
etiam magistris Cuthberto Tunstall, Roberto Wodwarde, Gabriele
Silvester et Johanne Aylove, superius specificatis, ac pluribus aliis,
comparuerunt personaliter Willelmus Baker de Crainbroke, Willelmus
Olberde de Godmersham, Robertus Reignold de Crainbroke et Thomas
Felde de Boxley. Et tunc ibidem abiurarunt omnem heresim et erroneas
suas opiniones contra fidem catholicam et ecclesie determinationem
quas tunc ibidem se tenuisse et docuisse confessi sunt, iuxta formam et
contenta in scedulis suarum abiurationum per eos et eorum quemlibet
publice et seriatim recitatis et per eosdem signo crucis signatis. Et
iuramentum prestiterunt corporale de perimplendo penitenciam eis et
eorum cuilibet per dictum reverendissimum patrem assignandam.
Quarum scedularum tenores sequuntur videlicet.

Abjuration of William Baker. In[a] the name of God, Amen. Bifore you,
the moost reverend fader in God my lord William archibisshop of
Caunterbury, I, William Baker of Crainbroke of yor diocise of
Caunterbury, of my pure hart and free will confesse and knowlege that
I in tymes passed bifore this houre, that is to witte by the space of . . .[b]
yeres and more, have beleved, thought, said, holden and affermed of
the sacraments of the churche and of the articles of the faith otherwise
than the holy churche of Rome and universall church of God techeth,
holdeth and obserueth. And many and divers open and damned errors
and heresies contrary to the true and catholik faith and determinacion
of holy churche I have bothe secretly and openly holden, beleued,
affermed and taught. And specially among other, thies errors and
heresies folowing, that is to witte:
Furst, that the blissed sacrament of the aulter ys not Crists very body,
flesshe and bloode, but oonly materiall bred, affermyng that God made
man but man cowde not make Gode.
Also that goyng in pilgremages unto holy and devoute places is not
profitable nor meritoriouse for mannys soule, and that labor and money
spent therabout ys but lost and doon in vayn.
Also that worshipping of images of seynts is not to be doon nor
profitable.

---

[a] Willelmus Baker *in margin.*   [b] *Blank space in MS.*

Wherfore I, the forsaid William Baker, willing heraftir to beleve in the faith of Criste and of his churche and to folow the true doctryne of holy churche, with a pure hert forsake and utterly despise my said errors, heresies and damnable opynions and confesse theym to be contraryous and repugnaunt to the faith of Criste and determinacion of his holy churche. And therfore the said errors, heresies and opinions in especiall and all other errors and heresies, fals doctrynes and damned opinions in generall likewise contrary and repugnaunt to the faith of Criste and determinacion of his church aforsaid I abjure, forsake and utterly renownce here bifore yor gracious lordship and all the honorable audience here assembled. And over that I swere by thies holy evangelies by me bodily here touched that from hensforth I shall never holde, teche, beleve or afferme the forsaid errors, heresies and damnable opinions nor noon other ayenst the faith of Criste holy church and determinacion of the same. Nor yet I shall by myself or any other persone pryvatly or apertly defende, maynteyn, socor, favor or support any persone that to my knowlege holdeth, beleveth, affermeth or techith any suche error, heresie or damned opinion nor any persone that is suspect of the same. And if I may knowe hereaftir any persone of suche error, heresie or of any suche fals doctrynes or any opinions contrary to the commen doctryne of the churche aforsaid, or if I may knowe any of their fautours, comforters, concelors or defensours or any that have suspect books or quayers of suche errors, heresies and damnable opinions, I shall withoute delaye geve knowlege unto yor goode lordshipp or to your successours or unto the ordinarie or ordinaries of the same persones or ells unto yor and their officers. Soo God me helpe and holy dome [fo. 162v] and thies holy evangelies.

In wittnes wherof to thies presents with myn owne hand I have made and subscribed the signe of the holy crosse. William Baker +

Abjuration of William Olberde junior and Robert Reignold. In[c] the name of God, Amen. Bifore you, the most reverent fader in God my lorde William archibisshop of Caunterbury, I, William Olberde junior of Godmersham, and I, Robert Reignold of Crainbroke, of yor diocise of Caunterbury, of my pure hert and free will confesse and knowlege that I in tymes passed bifore this houre, that is to witte by the space of vii yeres and more, have beleved, thought, said, holden, affermed and taught of the sacraments of the churche and of the articles of the faith otherwise than the holy church of Rome and universall churche of God techith, holdeth and observeth. And many and divers open and damned errors and heresies contrary to the true and catholik faith and determinacion of holy churche I

---

[c] Willelmus Olberd, Robertus Reignolde *in margin.*

have bothe secretly and openly holden, beleved, affermed and taught. And specially among other, thies errores and heresies folowing, that is to witte.

Furst, that the sacrament of the aulter ys not Crists very body but materiall bred.

Also that goyng in pilgremages unto holy and devoute places ys not profitable nor meritorious for mannys soule, and that labor and money spent therabout ys but lost and doon in vayne.

Also that the images of the crucifixe, of our blissed Lady and of other holy seynts of heven be not to be worshipped.

Wherfore I, the forsaid William Olberd, and Robert Reignold, willing hereaftir to beleve in the faith of Crist and of his churche and to folowe the true doctryne of holy churche, with a pure hert forsake and utterly despise my said errors, heresies and damnable opinions and confesse theym to be contraryous and repugnaunt to the faith of Crist and determinacion of his holy church. And therfore the said errors, heresies and opinions in especiall and all other errors and heresies, fals doctrynes and damned opinions in generall likewise contrary and repugnaunt to the faith of Criste and determinacion of his churche aforsaid I abjure, forsake and utterly renownce here bifore yor gracious lordship and all the honorable audience here assembled. And over that I swere by thies holy evangelies by me bodily here towched that from hensforth I shall never holde, teche, beleve or afferme the forsaid errors, heresies and damnable opinions nor noon other ayenst the faith of Criste holy churche and determinacion of the same. Nor yet I shall by my self or any other personne pryvatly or apertly defende, maynteyne, socour, favor or support any persone that to my knowlege holdeth, beleveth, affermeth or techith any suche error, heresies or damned opinions nor any persone that is suspect of the same. And if I may knowe hereaftir any persone of suche error, heresie or of any suche fals doctrynes or any opinions contrary to the commen doctryne of the church aforesaid, or if I may knowe any of their fautors, comfortors, concelors or defensors or any that have suspect books or quayers of suche errors, heresies and damnable opinions, I shall withoute delaye yeve knowlege unto yor good lordship or to your successours or unto the ordinary or ordinaries of the same persones or ells unto yor and their officers. Soo God me helpe and holy dome and thies holy evangelies.

In wittnes wherof to thies presents with myn owne hand I have made and subscribed the signe of the holy crosse. Willelmus Olberd junior + Robertus Reynold +

Abjuration of Thomas Felde. In[d] the name of God, Amen. Byfore you, the most reverent fader in God my lord William archiebisshop of

---

[d] Thomas Felde *in margin.*

Caunterbury, I, Thomas Feld of Boxley of yor diocise of Caunterbury, of my pure hert and free will confesse and knowlege that I bifore this at divers and sondry tymes and places have assisted and been present in the companyngs of suche persones as have rede, taught, comyned, holden and affermed divers errors, heresies and damnable opinions, that is to say.

Ayenst the blissed sacrament of the aulter, that it is not the very body of Criste, flesshe and bloode, but oonly materiall bred.

And that pilgremages to holy and devout places and offeryng and worshipping of images of the crucifixe and holy seynts were nothing profitable to mannys soule.

With other damnable opinions and heresies repugnaunt and contrary to the true and catholike faith of Crist and determinacion of holy church.

All the whiche damnable doctrynes, teching, commenyng, reding and affermyng of the said damnable heresies, and also the persones soo teching and affermyng, I have personally assisted, favored, conceled, supported and therunto consentid withoute any contradiccion to the same, contrary to Cristen faith and the determinacion and doctrine of holy churche.

Wherfore I, the forsaid Thomas Feld, willing hereaftir to beleve in the faith of Criste and of his churche and to folowe the true doctryne of holy churche, with a pure hert forsake and utterly despise my said errours, heresies and damnable opinions and confesse theym to be contraryous and repugnaunt to the faith of Crist and determinacion of his holy churche. And therfor the saide errors, heresies and opinions in especiall and all other errors and heresies, fals doctrynes and dampned opinions in generall lykewise contrary and repugnaunt to the faith of Crist and determinacion of his church aforsaid I, the forsaid Thomas, swere by thies holy evangelies by me bodyly here touched that from hensforth I, the forsaid Thomas, shall never holde, teche, bileve or afferme the said errors, heresies and damnable opinions nor noon other ayenst the faith of Crists holy churche and determynacion of the same. Nor yet I shall by meself or any other persone privatly or apertly defende, maynteyn, socor, favor or support any persone that to my knowlege holdeth, beleveth, affermeth or techith any suche errours, heresies or damned opinions nor any persone that is suspect of the same. And if I may knowe hereaftir any persone of suche error, heresie or of any suche fals doctrynes or any opinions contrary to the commen doctryne of the church aforsaid, or if I may know any of their fautors, comfortors, concelors or defensors or any that have suspect books or quayers of suche errors, heresies and damnable opinions, I shall without delaye geve knowlege unto yor goode lordship or to yor successors or unto the ordinary or ordinaries of the same persons or ells unto yor and their officers. So God me helpe and holy dome and holy evangelies.

In wittnes wherof to thies presents with myn owne hand I have made and subscribed the signe of the holy crosse. Thomas Felde +

Their penances. Et deinde reverendissimus pater iniunxit eisdem Willelmo Baker, Willelmo Olberd junior, Roberto Reignolde et Thome Felde penitenciam infrascriptam.

Primo quod die Dominica proxima in ecclesiis suis parochialibus incedant, more penitencium, ante crucem in processione cum fasciculis ligneis super humeris suis – nudi capita, tibias et pedes – et post processionem stabunt cum huiusmodi fasciculis ligneis ante ostium chori usque ad finem magne misse.

Item quod non se amoveant a locis ubi nunc inhabitant ad alias parochias etc., nisi prius certificent eundem reverendissimum patrem aut suos successores de loco ubi manere intendunt.

Item quod eorum quilibet apportabit dicto reverendissimo patri aut suis huiusmodi successoribus indilate libros, si quos de heresi habuerint.

Item si aliquas personas noverint suspectas de heresi aut libros de heresi habentes, certificent eundem reverendissimum patrem indilate.

Insuper dominus etc. iniunxit prefatis Willelmo Baker et Roberto Reignold quod eorum quilibet gestabit fasciculum depictum in sinistro humero vestimenti sui superioris durante vita eorum, nisi aliter fuerit dispensatum cum eisdem in ea parte modo superius specificato.

11. ABJURATION AND PENANCE OF JOAN OLBERDE OF GODMERSHAM, 3 JUNE, 1511 [fo. 163R]

Her appearance in court etc. Tercio die mensis Junii, anno Domini et loco immediate predictis,[1] coram prefato reverendissimo patre judicialiter pro tribunali sedente, presentibus tunc ibidem venerabilibus viris magistris Cuthberto Tunstall, utriusque iuris, Gabriele Silvester, Johanne Clement, Thoma Wellys, sacre pagine, Petro Potkyn et Johanne Kedwelly,[2] legum, doctoribus, et aliis, comparuit personaliter Johanna Olberde de Godmersham. Ac omnes hereses et errores fidei catholice et determinacioni ecclesie repugnantes abiuravit in genere et in specie, iuxta contenta in quadam scedula abiurationis sue huiumodi per eam tunc ibidem de verbo ad verbum recitata et manu sua signo crucis signata: prestito per eandem de peragendo penitenciam sibi per dictum reverendissimum patrem in ea parte iniungendam, ad sancta Dei evangelia per eam corporaliter tacta, iuramento[a] corporali. Cuius scedule tenor sequitur videlicet.

Her abjuration. In[b] the name of God, Amen. Bifore you, the most reverend fader in God my lord William archibisshop of Caunterbury, I, Johanne Olberde the wif of William Olberd the elder of Godmersham of yor diocise of Caunterbury, of my pure hert and free will confesse and knowlege that in tymes passed bifore this houre, that is to wite by the space of . . .[c] yeres and more, have beleved, thought, said, holden, affermed and taught of the sacraments of the churche and of the articles of the faith otherwise than the holy churche of Rome and universall church of God techeth, holdeth and observeth. And many and divers open and damned errors and heresies contrary to the true and catholik faith and determinacion of holy churche I have both secretly and openly holden, beleved, affermed and taught. And specially among other, thies errors and heresies folowing, that is to witte.

Furst, that the sacrament of the aulter is not Crists verey body but materiall bred.

Also that pilgremages to holy and devoute places be not necessary nother meritorious for mannys soule.

Also that worshipping of images of seynts is not to be doon nor profitable for mannys soule.

Also that a man shuld not pray to seynts but oonly to God.

Wherfore I, the forsaid Johanne, willing herafter to beleve in the

---

[1] See above, 65.
[2] See *BRUO*, ii, 1066, John Kydwelly.

---

[a] *MS.* iuramenti. [b] Johanna Olberd *in margin.* [c] *Blank space in MS.*

faith of Criste and of his churche and to folowe the very true doctryne of holy churche, with a pure hert forsake and utterly dispise my saide errors, heresies and damnable opinions and confesse theym to be contrarious and repugnaunt to the faith of Criste and determinacion of his holy churche. And therfore the said errors, heresies and opinions in especiall and all other errors and heresies, fals doctrynes and damned opinions in generall likewise contrary and repugnant to the faith of Crist and detemynacion of the churche aforsaid I abjure, forsake and utterly renownce here bifore yor gracious lordship and all the honorable audience here assembled. And over that I swere by thies holy evangelies by me bodily here touched that from hensforth I shall never holde, teche, bileve or afferme the forsaid errors, heresies and damnable opinions nor noon other ayenst the faith of Crists holy churche and determinacion of the same. Nor yet I shall by myself or any other persone pryvatly or apertly defende, maynteyn, socour, favor or support any persone that to my knowlege holdeth, beleveth, affermith or techeth any such error, heresie or damned opinion nor any persone that is suspect of the same. And if I may know thereaftir any persone of suche error, heresie or of any suche fals doctrines or any opinions contrary to the comen doctrine of the churche aforsaid, or if I may knowe any of their fautors, comfortors, concelors or defensors or any yat have suspect books or quayers of suche errors, heresies and damnable opinions, I shall without delay geve knowlege unto yor good lordship or to yor successors or unto the ordinarie or ordinaries of the same persons or ells unto yor and their officers. So God me helpe and holy dome and thies holy evangelies.

In wittnes wherof to thies presents with myn owne hand I have made and subscribed the signe of the holy crosse. Johanna Olberde +

Her penance. Et deinde, iuxta et secundum criminis qualitatem, idem reverendissimus pater tunc ibidem tulit sententiam in scriptis contra eandem diffinitivam, per quam ipsam Johannam Olberde perpetuis carceribus mancipandam fore decrevit quousque idem reverendissimus pater aut successores sui duxerint eandem fore relaxandam.

Et insuper tunc ibidem idem reverendissimus pater iniunxit eidem Johanne penitentiam infrascriptam videlicet. Quod incedat in publico mercato civitatis Cantuariensis die Sabbati proximo, induta sola camisia et uno lintheamine, gestans fasciculum ligneum in humero suo, circuiens mercatum. Et etiam in die Penthecostes[3] proxime futuro, simili modo gestabit fasciculum ligneum ante processionem in ecclesia cathedrali Cantuariense modo quo supra. Et deinde simili modo

---

[3] Pentecost Sunday, which was on 8 June in 1511.

consimilem peraget penitentiam in ecclesia sua parochiali diebus sancte Trinitatis et Corporis Christi[4] proxime ex tunc sequentibus, et stabit in medio ecclesie gestans huiusmodi fasciculum usque ad finem misse.

Insuper dominus iniunxit eidem quod gestabit fasciculum depictum super manica sinistra vestimenti sui superioris durante vita sua publice absque aliqua occultatione, nisi aliter fuerit dispensatum secum per dictum reverendissimum patrem aut suos successores.

Et insuper quod certificabit eundem reverendissimum patrem de peracta penitencia citra festum nativitatis sancti Johannis Baptiste,[5] et quod compareat personaliter coram eodem reverendissimo patre citra idem festum ad recipiendam residuam partem penitencie.

---

[4] Trinity Sunday, which was on 15 June in 1511, and the feast of Corpus Christi, which was kept on the following Thursday.

[5] 24 June, feast of the birthday of St. John the Baptist.

12. ABJURATION AND PENANCE OF ELIZABETH WHITE OF CANTERBURY,
3 JUNE, 1511 [fo. 163R–V]

Her appearance in court etc. Eisdem die et loco coram eodem reverendissimo patre etc. in presentia supradictorum testium,[1] comparuit personaliter Elizabeth White civitatis Cantuarie. Et abiuravit omnes hereses et errores per eam confessatos in specie ac omnes alios hereses et errores in genere, prout continetur in scedula sue abiurationis per eam seriatim recitata et manu sua signo crucis signata: iurata primitus ad sancta Dei evangelia de peragendo penitentiam sibi in ea parte iniungendam. Cuius scedule tenor sequitur videlicet.

Her abjuration. In[a] the name of God, Amen. Bifore you, the most reverend fader in God my lord William archiebisshop of Caunterbury, I, Elizabeth White of your citie of Caunterbury, of my pure hert and free will confesse and knowlege that I in tymes passed bifore this houre, that ys to witte by the space of . . . [b] yeres and more, have beleveth, thought, said, holden, affirmed and taught of the sacraments of the church and of the articles of the faith otherwise than the holy church of Rome and universall church of God techeth, holdeth and observeth. And many and diverse open and damned errors and heresies contrary to the true and catholike feith and determinacion of holy churche I have bothe secretly and openly holden, beleved, affirmed and taught. And specially among other, thies errors and heresies folowing, that is to witte.

First, that the blissed sacrament of the aulter is not Crists verey body but oonly materiall brede.

Also that pilgremages to holy and devoute places be not necessary nor meritorious for mannys soule, but that money and labour doon and spent therabout ys all in vayne.

Also that worshipping of images of the holy crucifixe, of our blissed Lady and of other seynts is not to be doon nor profitable for mannys soule.

Wherfore I, the forsaid Elizabeth[c] White, willing hereaftir to beleve in the faith of Crist and of his churche and to folowe the true doctrine of holy churche, with a pure hert forsake and utterly despise my said errours, heresies and damnable opinions and confesse theym to be contrarious and repugnaunt to the faith of Criste and determinacion of his holy churche. And therfore the saide errors, heresies and opinions in especiall and all other errors and heresies, fals doctrynes and damned opinions in generall likewise contrary and re[fo. 163v]pugnaunt to the faith of Criste and determinacion of his churche aforesaid I abjure, forsake and utterly

---

[1] See above, 70.

[a] Elizabeth White *in margin.*   [b] *Blank space in MS.*   [c] MS. Johanne.

renownce here bifore yor gracious lordship and all the honourable audience here assembled. And over that I swere by thies holy evangelies by me bodily here touched that from hensforth I shall never holde, teche, beleve or afferme the forsaid errors, heresies and damnable opinions nor none other ayenst the faith of Cristes holy church and determinacion of the same. Nor yet I shall by myself or any other persone that to my knowlege holdeth, beleveth, affermeth or techeth any suche error, heresie or damned opynion nor any persone that is suspect of the same. And if I may knowe hereaftir any persone of suche erroure, heresie or of any suche fals doctrynes or any opinions contrary to the comen doctryne of the churche aforesaid, or if I may knowe any of their fautors, comfortors, concelors or defensors or any that have suspect books or quayers of suche errors, heresies and damnable opinions, I shall withoute delay geve knowlege unto yor goode lordshipp or to yor successors or unto the ordinary or ordinaries of the same persones or ells unto yor and their officers. Soo God me helpe and holy dome and thies holy evangelies.

In wittnes wherof to thies presents with myn owne hand I have made and subscribed the signe of the holy crosse. Elizabeth White +

Her penance. Cui idem reverendissimus pater iniunxit quod die Penthecostes[2] proxime futuro locum mercati civitatis Cantuarie incedat, induta sola camisia et uno lintheamine, gestans fasciculum ligneum super humero suo.

Item quod die Penthecostes proximo antecedat processionem in ecclesia cathedrali Cantuariense, induta solomodo camisia et tunica, Anglice a kyrtell, gestans fasciculum ligneum super humero suo, et post processionem ipsum fasciculum ibidem relinquet.

Item die sancte Trinitatis[3] proxime ex tunc sequente, simili modo induta, nuda pedibus et tibiis, in ecclesia sua parochiali similem penitenciam peraget etc.

Item quod gestabit fasciculum depictum super manica sinistra vestimenti sui superioris durante vita sua publice absque aliqua occultatione, nisi aliter fuerit dispensatum secum per dictum reverendissimum patrem aut suos successores.

Item quod non amovebit se a parochia ubi iam inhabitat, nisi prius certificabit eundem reverendissimum patrem seu eius successores de loco ubi manere intendit.

Item quod revelabit quoscumque suspectos de heresi aut libros de heresi habentes.

Item quod perimplebit quamlibet particulam huiusmodi iniunctionis sub pena relapsus.

[2] See above, 71, note 3.
[3] See above, 72, note 4.

13. ABJURATION AND PENANCE OF AGNES RAYNOLD OF CRANBROOK, 26 JULY, 1511 [fo. 163V]

Her appearance in court etc. Vicesimo sexto die Julii anno Domini supradicto in capella dicti reverendissimi patris apud Knoll, coram eodem reverendissimo patre pro tribunali iudicialiter sedente, presentibus tunc ibidem magistro Cuthberto Tunstall, utriusque iuris doctore, eiusdem reverendissimi patris cancellario, ac magistris Willelmo Potkyn et David Cooper, notariis publicis, et aliis, comparuit personaliter Agnes Reignold de Cranebroke. Et abiuravit omnes hereses et opiniones damnatas determinationi universalis ecclesie et fidei catholice contrarias, iuxta et secundum contenta in scedula abiurationis sue eidem publice tunc ibidem perlecta ac per eam recitata ac manu eiusdem signo crucis signata: prestito primitus per eandem de peragendo penitentiam sibi per dictum reverendissimum patrem in ea parte iniungendam, ad sancta Dei evangelia per eam corporaliter tacta, iuramento corporali. Cuius scedule tenor sequitur.

Her abjuration. In[a] the name of God, Amen. Bifore you, moost reverend fader in God my lord William Archiebisshop of Caunterbury, I, Agnes Raynold of Crainbroke, lately servant with William Baker and now servant with oon Jervis Henly, knowleging myself to be of yor diocise of Caunterbury, of my pure here and free will confesse that bifore[b] this daye at diverse tymes and places [I] have assisted and been present where as it hath be comyned, rede, taught, holden and affermed and I have consentid therto:

That the blissed sacrament of the aulter ys not the very body of Crist, flesshe and bloode, but oonly materiall brede.

And that pilgremages to holy and devoute places, and offeryng and worshipping of images of the crucifixe and holy seynts, were nothing profitable to mannys soule.

With other damnable opinions and heresies repugnant and contrary to the true and catholik faith of Crist and determinacion of the holy churche.

The whiche all damnable doctrines, heresies and also thoo persones so teching and affermyng I have personally assisted, favoured, conceled, supported and therunto consentid without any contradiccion to the same, contrary to cristen faith and the determinacion and doctryne of the church.

Wherfore I, the said Agnes, willing hereaftir to beleve in the faith of Criste and of his church and to folowe the true doctryne of holy churche,

---

[a] Agnes Raynold *in margin.*
[b] that bifore *repeated after* bifore.

75

with a pure hert and free will forsake and utterly despise my said errors,
heresies and damnable opinions and confesse them to be contrarius and
repugnaunt to the faith of Criste and determinacion of his holy churche.
And therfore the said heresies, errors and damned opinions in especiall
and all other errors and heresies, fals doctrynes and damned opinions in
generall likewise contrary and repugnaunt to the faith of Criste and
determinacion of his churche forsaid I, the forsaid Agnes, abjure, forsake
and utterly renownce here before yor gracious lordship and all the
honourable audience here assembled. And over that I, the forsaid Agnes,
swere by thies holy evangelies by me bodily touched that from hensforth
I shall never holde, teche, bileve or afferme the saide errors, heresies and
damnable opinions nother noon other ayenst the faith of Crist, holy
churche and the determinacion of the same. Nother yet I shall by myself
or any other persone privatly or apertly defende, maynteyne, socour,
favor or support any persone that to my knowlege holdeth, beleveth,
affermeth or techeth any suche errors, heresies and damnable opinions
contrary to the comen doctrine of the holy church forsaid nor any
persone that is suspecte of the same. And if I may knowe hereaftir any
persone of suche errors, heresies or of suche fals doctrines or any
opinions contrary to the said doctryne of the churche, or if I may knowe
any of their fautors, comforters, concelors or defenders or any that have
suspect books or quayers of suche errors, heresies and damned opinions,
I shall withoute delaye geve knowlege unto yor good lordship or to yor
successors or unto the ordinarie or ordinaries of thoo same persones or
elles unto yor or their officers. Soo God me helpe and holy dome and
thies holy evangelies.

In wittnes wherof to thies presents with myn owne hand I have made
and subscribed the signe of the holy crosse. Agnes Raynold +

Her penance. Et tunc ibidem ipse reverendissimus pater iniunxit eidem
Agneti quod amodo non utatur veste linea, Anglice a smokk, aliquo die
Veneris durante vita eiusdem, nisi dies natalis Domini[1] contingat eodem
die Veneris. Et quolibet die Veneris dicat v Pater noster, quinque Ave et
unum Credo pro penitentia eidem iniuncta propter heresim.

---

[1] Christmas day, 25 December.

14. ABJURATION AND PENANCE OF THOMAS CHURCHE OF GREAT CHART, 29 JULY, 1511 [fos. 163V-164R]

His appearance in court etc. Vicesimo nono mensis Julii anno Domini supradicto in ecclesia parochiali de Sevenoke etc., coram prefato reverendissimo patre pro tribunali iudicialiter sedente, presentibus tunc ibidem magistro Cuthberto Tunstall, utriusque iuris doctore, eiusdem reverendissimi patris cancellario, ac magistris Willelmo Potkyn et David Cooper, notariis publicis, et aliis, comparuit personaliter tunc ibidem Thomas Churche de Charte Magna. Et modo quo supra omnes hereses abiuravit in forma contenta in scedula sue abiurationis eidem publice lecta et per eum ibidem verbatim recitata et manu sua signo crucis signata: prestito primitus per eundem de paragendo penitenciam sibi per dictum reverendissimum patrem in ea parte iniungendam, ad sancta Dei evangelia per eum corporaliter tacta, iuramento corporali.

His abjuration. In^a the name of God, Amen. Bifore you, the most reverend fader in God my lord William archiebisshop of Caunterbury, I, Thomas Churche of the parisshe of Greate Charte of yor diocise of Caunterbury, of my pure hert and free will confesse and knowlege that I [fo. 164r] bifore this at diverse tymes and places have assisted and been present in the companyng of suche persones as have rede, taught, comyned, holden and affermed divers errours, heresies and damnable opinions, that is to say.

Agaynst the sacrament of baptisme, that it was nothing profitable to mannys soule.

And that the sacrament of confession was of noon effect, and that preests hadde made it of their owne invencion.

Item that the solemnisacion of matrimony was not necessary, nother the sacrament of extreme unccion, for mannys soule.

And that the blissed sacrament of the aulter was not Godds body but oonly materiall brede.

Item that goyng at pilgremage and worshipping of images was noo profite.

With other damnable opinions and heresies repugnaunt and contrary to the true and catholik faith of Crist and determynacion of the holy church.

The whiche all damnable doctrynes, techings, comenyngs, redings and affirmyngs of the said damnable errors and heresies, and all thoo persones soo teching and affermyng, I have personally assisted, favored, conceled, supported and to all the forsaid heresies consentid without any contradiccion to the same, contrary to cristen faith and the determinacion of holy churche.

---

^a Thomas Churche *in margin.*

Wherfore I, the forsaid Thomas, willing heraftir to beleve in the feith of Crist and of his churche and to folow the true doctryne of holy church, with a pure hert forsake and utterly despise my said errores, heresies and damned opinions and confesse theym to be contrarious and repugnaunt to the faith of Crist and the determinacion of his holy churche. And therfore the said errors, heresies and damned opinions in especiall and all other errors, heresies, fals doctrines and damned opinions in generall likewise contrary and repugnaunt to the faith of Criste and determinacion of his churche forsaid I, the forsaid Thomas, abjure, forsake and utterly renownce here bifore yor gracious lordship and all the honorable audience here assembled. And over that I, the forsaid Thomas, swere by thies holy evangelies by me here bodily touched that from hensforth I shall never holde, teche, beleve or afferme the saide errors, heresies and damned opinions nor noon other agaynst the faith of Cristes holy churche and determinacion of the same. Nor yet I shall by myself or any other persone pryvatly or apertly defende, maynteyn, socor, favor or support any persone that to my knowlege holdeth, beleveth, affermeth and techeth any suche errors, heresies or damned opinions nor any persone that is suspect of the same. And if I may knowe hereaftir any persone of suche errors, heresies or of any suche fals doctrynes or any opinions contrary to the comen doctryne of the churche forsaid, or if I may knowe any of their fautors, comfortors, concelors or defenders or any that have suspect books or quayers of suche errors, heresies and damned opinions, I shall without delay geve knowlege unto yor goode lordship or to yor successors or unto the ordinary or ordinaries of the same persones or ellys unto yor or their officers. So God me helpe and holy dome and thies holy evangelies.

In wittnes wherof to thies presents with myn owne hand I have made and subscribed the signe of the holy crosse. Thomas Church +

His penance. Et deinde tunc ibidem ipse reverendissimus pater iniunxit eidem Thome pro penitencia quod tribus diebus Dominicis proxime futuris gestabit fasciculum ligneum, sedens super crucem in cimiterio ecclesie de Charte predicte, dummodo processio fiat circa idem cimiterium; et quod immediate post processionem adducatur in navem ecclesie et ibidem publice expectabit, gestans huiusmodi fasciculum usque ad finem misse.

Et insuper quod gestabit fasciculum depictum in humero sinistro super manica vestimenti sui superioris durante vita sua, publice absque aliqua occultatione, nisi aliter fuerit secum dispensatum per dictum reverendissimum patrem aut suos successores.

Et quod non mutabit locum mansionis sue a parochia ubi iam inhabitat absque licentia dicti reverendissimi patris aut suorum successsorum, sub pena relapsus.

15. ABJURATIONS AND PENANCES OF ALICE HILLES OF TENTERDEN AND MARGARET BAKER OF CRANBROOK, 2 AUGUST, 1511 [fo. 164R–V]

Their appearance in court etc. Item secundo die mensis Augusti anno Domini quo supra in ecclesia sive capella curata de Otford etc., coram prefato reverendissimo patre pro tribunali iudicialiter sedente, presentibus tunc ibidem magistro Cuthberto Tunstall, utriusque iuris doctore, eiusdem reverendissimi patris cancellario, ac magistris Willelmo Potkyn et David Cooper, notariis publicis, et aliis, comparuerunt personaliter Alicia Hilles, filia Roberti Hilles, de Tenterden, et Margareta Baker, uxor Willelmi Baker, de Cranebroke. Ac omnes hereses et damnatas opiniones iuri divino et ecclesie universalis determinationi repugnantes et contrarias abiurarunt, iuxta contenta in scedulis suarum abiurationum eis publice perlectis et per eas publice recitatis tunc ibidem, quas signo crucis earum utraque signavit manibus propriis: prestitio primitus per easdem et earum quamlibet de peragendo penitenciam eis et earum cuilibet per dictum reverendissimum patrem in ea parte iniungendam, ad sancta Dei evangelia per earum utrasque corporaliter tacta, iuramento corporali. Quarum scedularum tenores sequuntur videlicet.

Abjuration of Alice Hilles. In[a] the name of God, Amen. Bifore you, most reverend fader in God my lord William archiebisshop of Caunterbury, I, Alice Hilles, the doughter of Robert Hilles of Tenterden of the age of xx[ti] yeres and of yor diocise of Caunterbury, of my free will and pure hert confesse and knowlege that I, bifore this at diverse tymes and places, have assisted and been present in the company of suche persones as have redde, taught, commyned, holden and affermed divers errors, heresies and damnable opinions. And I myself have beleved in thoes same, that is to say.

That the holy sacrament of the aulter was not Godds body but oonly holy brede.

And that confession was not profitable for mannys soule, and that a preest had noo power to absoyle a man of his synnes, and therfore a man shuld confesse hymself oonly to God.

And I beleved that it was nought to goo on pilgremages and to worship images of seynts.

And of all thies heresies I was never shriven, but consentid to the forsaid heresies with other damnable opinions repugnaunt and contrary to the true and catholik faith of Crist and determynacion of holy churche.

---

[a] Alicia Hilles *in margin.*

All the which damnable doctrynes, techings, commenyngs, redings and affermyngs and beleving of the said heresies, and also the persones so teching and affermyng, I have personally assisted, favored, conceled, supported and therunto consentid without any contradicion to the same, contrary to Crists faith and the determynacion and doctryne of holy churche.

Wherfore I, the forsaid Alice, willing hereaftir to beleve in the faith of Crist and of his churche and to folowe the true doctrine of holy churche, with a pure hert forsake and utterly dispise my said errors, heresies and damnable opinions and confesse theym to be contrarious and repugnaunt to the faith of Crist and the determinaicon of his holy church. And therfore the said errors, heresies and damned opinions in especiall and all other errors, heresies, fals doctrines and damned opinions in generall likewise contrary and repugnaunt to the faith of Crist and determinacion of his churche forsaid I, the forsaid Alice, abjure, forsake and utterly renownce here bifore yor gracious lordship and all the honorable audience here assembled. And over that I, the forsaid Alice, swere by thies holy evangelies by me here bodily toched that from hensforth I shall never holde, teche, beleve or afferme the said errors, heresies and damned opinions nor noon other agaynst the faith of Crists holy churche and the determinaicon of the same. Nor yet I shall by myself or any other persone pryvatly or apertly defende, maynteyne, favor, socor or support any persone that to my knowlege holdeth, beleveth, affermeth, techeth any suche errors, heresies or damned opinions nor any persone that is suspect of the same. And if I may know hereaftir any persone of suche errors, heresies or damned opinions or any persone that is suspect of the same, and if I may know hereaftir any persone of suche errors, heresies or of any suche fals doctrines or any opinions contrary to the commen doctrine of the churche forsaid, or if I may know any of their fautors, confortors, concelors or defenders or any that have suspect books or quayers of suche errors, heresies and damnable opinions, I shall without delay yeve knowlege unto yor goode lordship or to yor successors or unto the ordinary or ordinaries of thoes same persones or elles to yor or their officers. So God me helpe and holy dome and thies holy evanglies.

In wittnes wherof to thies presents with myn owne hand I have made and subscribed [fo. 164v] the signe of the holy crosse. Alice Hilles +

Abjuration of Margaret Baker. In[b] the name of God, Amen. Bifore you, most reverend fader in God my lord William archiebisshop of Caunterbury, I, Margaret Baker, wif of William Baker of Cranebroke of

---

[b] Margareta Baker *in margin.*

yor diocise of Canterbury, of my pure hert and free will confesse and knowlege that I bifore this at divers tymes and places have assisted and ben present in the company of suche persones as have rede, taught, commyned, holden and affermed diverse errors, heresies and damnable [opinions] and I myselfe beleve in thoes same, that is to say.

That the sacrament of the aulter was not Crists body but oonly materiall brede.

And that a man shuld not utter his confession to a preest.

Also that worshipping of images of seynts and goyng a pilgremage was not profitable for mannys soule.

With other damnable opinions and heresies repugnaunt and contrary to the true and catholik faith of Crist and determinacion of holy church.

All the which damnable doctrynes, techings, commenyngs, redings and affermyngs and belyving of the said damnable opinions, and also the persones so teching and affermyng, I have personally assisted, favored, concelled, supported and therunto consentid without any contradicion to the same, contrary to cristen faith and the determinacion and doctryne of holy church.

Wherfore I, the forsaid Margaret, willing hereaftir to beleve in the faith of Criste and of his churche and to folowe the true doctrine of the same, with a pure hert forsake and utterly despise my said errours, heresies and damnable opinions and confesse theym to be contraryous and repugnaunt to the faith of Crist and the determiancion of his holy churche. And therfore the said errors, heresies and damned opinions in especiall and all other errors, heresies, fals doctrines and damned opinions in generall likewise contrary and repugnaunt to the faith of Crist and determiancion of his churche forsaid I, the forsaid Margaret, abjure, forsake and utterly renownce here bifore yor gracious lordship and the honorable audience here assembled. And over that I, the forsaid Margaret, swere by thies holy evangelies by me here bodily touched that from hensforth I shall never holde, teche, beleve or afferme the saide errors, heresies and damned opinions nor noon other agaynst the faith of Crists holy church and the determinacion of the same. Nor yet I shall by myself or any other persone pryvatly or apertly defende, maynteyn, favor, socor or support any opinions nor any persone that is suspected of the same. And if I may knowe hereaftir any persone of suche errors, heresies or of any suche fals doctrines or any contrary to the commen doctrine of the church forsaid, or if I may know any of their fautors, comfortors, concelors or defenders or any that have suspect books or quayers of suche errors, heresies and damned opinions, I shall without delay geve knowlege unto yor good lordship or to the ordinary or ordinaries of the same persones or elles to yor and their officers. So God me helpe and holy dome and by thies holy evangelies.

In wittnes wherof to the presents with myn owne hand I have made and subscribed the signe of the holy crosse. + Margaret Baker

Their penances. Deinde idem reverendissimus pater iniunxit eidem Alicie pro penitencia quod imposterum durante vita sua non utatur interula – videlicet a smoke – de veste linea aliquo die Veneris, nisi aliquod festum principale contingat eodem die. Et quolibet die Veneris huiusmodi dicat quinque Pater noster, quinque Ave Maria et unum Credo quamdiu vixerit.

Item tunc ibidem idem reverendissimus pater iniunxit prefate Margarete Baker quod se abstineat omni genere piscium quolibet die Veneris quamdiu vixerit: et dicat decies Pater noster, decies Ave Maria.

16. ABJURATION AND PENANCE OF VINCENT LYNCHE OF HALDEN,
3 AUGUST, 1511 [fos. 164V–165R]

His appearance in court etc. Item, tercio die mensis Augusti anno
Domini millesimo quingentesimo in ecclesia parochiali de Sevenoke
etc., coram prelibato reverendissimo patre pro tribunali iudicialiter
sedente, presentibus tunc ibidem magistro Cuthberto Tunstall, utriusque
iuris doctore, eiusdem reverendissimi patris cancellario, ac magistris
Willelmo Potkyn et David Cooper, notariis publicis, et aliis, comparuit
personaliter Vincentius Lynche de Halden. Et modo quo supra omnes
hereses, errores at damnatas opiniones fidei catholice et sancte matris
ecclesie determinationi repugnantes abiuravit publice, sub forma et
modo contentis in scedula sue abiurationis sibi publice perlecta et per
eum tunc ibidem verbatim recitata, quam scedulam manu sua propria
signo crucis signavit: prestito primitus per eundem de peragendo
penitenciam sibi per dictum reverendissimum patrem in ea parte
iniungendam, ad sancta Dei evangelia per eum corporaliter tacta,
iuramento corporali. Cuius scedule tenor sequitur videlicet.

His abjuration. In[a] the name of God, Amen. Bifore you, moost
reverend fader in God my lord William archiebisshop of Caunterbury, I,
Vincent Lynche of Halden of yor diocise of Canterbury, of my pure hert
and free will confesse and knowlege that I bifore this at divers tymes
and places have assisted and ben present in the company of suche
persones as have taught, commyned, holden and affermed diverse
errors, heresies and damnable opinions, that is to say.

That the sacrament of the aulter was not Crists body but oonly brede.

And that pilgremage was not profitable for mannys soule.

And also that images of seynts shuld not be worshipped.

With other damnable opinions and heresies repugnaunt and contrary
to the true and catholik faith of Crist and determinacion of the holy
churche.

The whiche all damnable doctrynes, techings, comenyngs, redings
and affirmyngs of the said damnable errors and heresies and also the
persones so teching and affermyng I have personally assisted, favoured,
conceled and supported and to the forsaid heresies consentid without
any contradiccion to the same, contrary to cristen faith and the
determinacion of holy churche.

Wherfore I, the foresaid Vincent, willing hereaftir to beleve in the
faith of Crist and to folowe the true doctryne of holy churche, with a
pure hert forsake and utterly despise my said heresies, errors and

[a] Vincentius Lynche *in margin.*

damnable opinions and confesse theym to be contrarius and repugnaunt of the faith of Crist and determinacion of his holy churche. And therfore the said errors, heresies and damned opinions in especiall and all other errors, heresies, fals doctrines and damned opinions in generall likewise contrary and repugnaunt to the faith of Crist and determinacion of his said churche I, the forsaid Vincent, abjure, forsake and utterly renownce here bifore yor gracious lordship and all the honorable audience here assembled. And over that I, the forsaid Vincent swere by thies holy evangelies by me here bodily touched that from hensforth I shall never hold, teche, beleve or afferme the said errors, heresies and damned opinions nor noon other ayenst the faith of Crist, holy churche and determinacion of the same. Nor yet I shall by myself or any other persone pryvatly or apertly defende, maynteyne, favor, socor or support any persone that to my knowlege holdeth, beleveth, affermeth or techeth any suche errors, heresies or damned opinions nor any persone that is suspect of the same. And if I may know hereaftir any persone that holdeth any suche errors, heresies or any suche fals doctrynes or any opinions contrary to the commen doctrine of the churche forsaid, or if I may know any of their fautors, comforters, concelors or defenders or any that have suspect books or quayers of suche errors, heresies and damned opinions I shall without delay geve knowlege unto yor good lordship or unto yor successors or unto the ordinarie or ordinaries of thoes same persones or elles to yor or their officers. So God me helpe and holy dome and thies holy evangelies.

In wittnes wherof to thies presents with myn owne hand I have made and subscribed the signe of the holy crosse. Vincent Lynche +

His penance. Cui quidem Vincentio Lynche prefatus reverendissimus pater iniunxit pro penitentia quod die Dominica proxima, die assumptionis beate Marie[1] et Dominica proxime ex tunc sequente – nudus tibias, pedes et caput – stabit ad fores cancelli ecclesie parochialis de Halden predict' immediate ante processionem, gestans fasciculum ligneum in humero suo. Exinde antecedat crucem in processione, [fo. 165r] gestans fasciculum ligneum circa cimiterium. Et post processionem stabit in navi ecclesie ante ostium cancelli, gestans huiusmodi fasciculum usque ad finem misse. Et ultimus exibit ecclesiam ipsis diebus.

Item quod non recedat a parochia de Halden, morandi causa, absque licentia a dicto reverendissimo patre obtenta aut suorum successorum, sub pena relapsus.

---

[1] 15 August, feast of the assumption of St. Mary.

17. ABJURATION AND PENANCE OF JOAN RICHE OF WITTERSHAM,
8 AUGUST, 1511 [fo. 165R]

Her appearance in court etc. Octavo die mensis Augusti anno Domini
supradicto in capella dicti reverendissimi patris infra manerium suum
de Knoll, coram eodem reverendissimo patre pro tribunali iudicialiter
sedente, presentibus magistris Cuthberto Tunstall, Gabriele Silvester,
Clemente Browne, doctoribus, ac Johanne Aylove, in legibus
bacallario, et aliis, comparuit personaliter Johanna Riche de Wittisham.
Et abiuravit omnes hereses et damnatas opiniones iuri divino et ecclesie
universalis determinationi repugnantes et contrarias, iuxta contenta in
scedula abiurationis sue eidem publice perlecta et per eam tunc ibidem
recitata ac signo crucis manu sua signata: prestito primitus per eandem
de peragendo penitentiam sibi per dictum reverendissimum patrem in
ea parte iniungendam, ad sancta Dei evangelia per eam corporaliter
tacta, iuramento corporali. Cuius scedule tenor sequitur videlicet.

Her abjuration. In[a] the name of God, Amen. Bifore you, most reverend
fader in God my lord William archiebisshop of Caunterbury, I, Jone
Riche of Wittisham of yor diocise of Caunterbury, of my pure hert and
free will confesse and knowlege that I bifore this att divers tymes and
places have assisted and ben present in the company of suche persones
as hath rede, taught, commenyd, holden and affermed divers errors,
heresies and damnable opinions and I myself have said hurd,
commynd, affermed and conceled the same, that is to say.
    That the blissed sacrament of the aulter was not Crists body but
oonly materiall brede.
    And that a prest hath noo power to assoile any man of his synnes and
that confession was not profitable.
    And also that images of the crucifixe, of our Lady and other seynts
aught not to be worshipped bicause they were made with mannys
hands, and that they were but stokks and stonys.
    And also that pilgremage was not profitable.
    With other damnable opinions and heresies repugnaunt and contrary
to the true and catholik faith of Crist and determinacion of holy
churche.
    All the whiche damnable doctrynes, techings, commynyngs, redings
and affermyngs of the said damnable heresies and also the persones so
teching and affermyng I have personally assisted, favored, conceled
and supported without any contradiccion to the same, contrary to
cristen faith and the determinacion and doctrine of holy churche.

---

[a] Johanna Riche *in margin.*

Wherfore I, the forsaid Johane, willing hereafter to beleve in the faith of Crist and of his churche and to folowe the true doctrine of holy churche, with a pure hert forsake and utterly despise my said errors, heresies and damnable opinions and confesse theym to be contraryous and repugnaunt to the faith of Criste and determinacion of his holy churche. And therefore the said errors, heresies and damnable opinions in especiall and all other errors and heresies, false doctrines and damned opinions in generall likewise contrary and repugnaunt to the faith of Criste and determinacion of his churche forsaid I, the forsaid Johane, abjure, forsake and utterly renownce here bifore yor gracious lordship and all the honorable audience here assembled. And over that I, the forsaid Johane, swere by thies holy evangelies by me here bodily toched that from hensforth I shall never holde, teche and afferme the said errors heresies and damned opinions nor noon other ayenst the faith of Crists holy churche and determinacion of the same. Nor yet I shall by myself or any other persone pryvatly or apertly defende, maynteyne, favor, socor or support any persone that to my knowlege holdeth, beleveth, affermeth or techeth any suche errors, heresies or damned opinions nor any persone that is suspected of the same. And if I may knowe hereaftir any persone of suche errors, heresies or of any suche false doctrynes or any opinions contrary to the commen doctrine of the churche aforsaid, or if I may knowe any of theire fautors, comfortors, concelers or defenders or any that have suspect books or quayers of suche errors, heresies and damned opinions, I shall without delay geve knowlege unto yor good lordship or to yor successors or unto the ordinary or ordinaries of the same persones or elles to yor or their officers. So God me helpe and holy dome and thies holy evangelies.

In wittnes wherof to thies presents with myn owne hand I have made and subscribed the signe of the holy crosse. Johane Riche +

Absolution from excommunication and penance. Et deinde idem reverendissimus pater eam absolvit a sentencia excommunicationis, quam premissorum pretextu incurrerat, et sacramentis ecclesie ac communioni fidelium restituit.

Et insuper tunc ibidem idem reverendissimus pater iniunxit eidem quod antecedat in processione die Dominica proxima in ecclesia parochiali de Wittisham – nuda tibias et pedes – gestans cereum valoris unius denarie, et quod offerat eundem tempore offertorii. Ac etiam quod nullo die Veneris dum vixerit utetur camisia sed induetur sola veste lanea, nisi in principalibus festis.

18. ABJURATIONS AND PENANCES OF JOHN LYNCHE OF TENTERDEN AND
THOMAS BROWNE OF CRANBROOK, 16 AUGUST, 1511 [fo. 165R–V]

Their appearance in court etc. Decimosexto die mensis Augusti anno
Domini supradicto in oratorio dicti reverendissimi patris infra
manerium suum de Knoll, presentibus tunc ibidem magistris Willelmo
Warham, archiepiscopo[a] Cantuariense, Cuthberto Tunstall, Thoma
Welles, Gabriele Silvester, utriusque iuris et sacre pagine doctoribus, ac
Thoma Milling et aliis, comparuerunt personaliter Johannes Lynche de
Tenterden et Thomas Browne de Cranebroke coram eodem reverendissimo patre. Et in forma superius recitata omnes hereses et errores
fidei catholice repugnantes, iuxta quod continetur in scedulis suarum
abiurationum per eos tunc ibidem publice recitatis et signo crucis
manibus suis signatis, abiurarunt et eisdem renunciarunt: prestito
primitus per eosdem et eorum utrumque de peragendo penitenciam eis
et alteri eorum per dictum reverendissimum patrem in ea parte iniungendam, ad sancta Dei evangelia per eos corporaliter tacta, iuramento
corporali. Quarum scedularum tenores sequuntur videlicet.

Abjuration of John Lynche. In[b] the name of God, Amen. Bifore you, the
most reverend fader in God my lord William archiebisshop of
Caunterbury, I, John Lynche of Tenterden of yor diocise of
Caunterbury, of my pure hert and free will confesse and knowlege that
I in tymes passed bifore this houre, that is to witte by the space of xx[ti]
yeres and more, have beleved, thought, said, holden, affermyd and
taught of the sacraments of the churche and of the articles of the faith
otherwise than the holy churche of Rome and universall churche of
God techeth, holdeth and observeth. And many and divers open and
damned errors and heresies contrary to the true and catholik faith and
determinacion of holy churche I have bothe secretly and openly holden,
beleved, affermed and taught. And specially among all other, thies
errors and heresies folowing, that is to witte.

First, that the blissed sacrament of the aulter is not Crists verey body
but oonly materiall brede.

Also that pilgremages to holy and devoute places be not necessary
nor meritorious for mannys soule but that money and labor doon and
spent thereaboute is all in vayn.

Also that worshipping of images of the holy crucifixe, of our blissed
Lady and of other seynts is not to be doon nor profitable for mannys soule.

Wherfore I, the forsaid John Lynche, willing hereaftir to beleve in the
faith of Criste and of his churche and to folowe the true doctryne of holy

---

[a] *MS.* arch'no.   [b] Johannes Lynche *in margin.*

church, with a pure hert forsake and utterly despise my said errors, heresies and damnable opinions and confesse them to be contraryous and repugnaunt to the faith of Criste and determinacion of his holy churche. And therfore the said errors, heresies and opinions in especiall and all other errors and heresies, fals doctrynes and[c] [fo. 165v] damned opinions in generall likewise contrary and repugnaunt to the faith of Criste and determinacion of his holy churche aforsaid I abjure, forsake and utterly renownce here bifore yor gracious lordship and all the honorable audience here assembled. And over that I swere by thies holy evangelies by me bodily here touched that frome hensforth I shall never holde, teche, beleve or afferme the said heresies, errours and damnable opinions nor noon other ayenst the feith of Criste, holy churche and determinacion of the same. Nor yet I shall by myself or any other persone pryvatly or apertly defende, maynteigne, socor, favor or support any persone that to my knowlege holdith, beleveth, affermeth or techeth any suche errors, heresye or damned opinions nor yet any persone that is suspect of the same. And if I may knowe hereaftir any persone of suche error, heresie or of any suche fals doctrynes or any opinions contrary to the comen doctrine of the churche aforsaid, or if I may knowe any of their fautors, comfortors or defensors or any that have suspect books or quayers of suche errors, heresies and damned opinions, I shall withoute delay geve knowlege unto yor good lordship and to yor successors or to the ordinarie or ordinaries of the same persones or elles unto yor and their officers. So God me helpe and holy dome and thies holy evangelies.

In wittnes wherof to thies presents with myn owne hande I have [made] and subscribed the signe of the holy crosse +

Abjuration of Thomas Browne. In[d] the name of God, Amen. Bifore you, most reverend fader in God my lord William archibisshop of Caunterbury, I, Thomas Browne of Cranebroke of yor diocise of Caunterbury, of my pure hert and free will confesse and knowlege that I in tymes passed bifore this houre, that ys to witte by the space of oon yere and more, have beleved, thought, said, holden, affermed and taught of the sacraments of the churche and of the articles of the faith otherwise than the holy churche of God techeth, holdeth and observeth. And many and divers open and damned errors and heresies contrary to the true and catholik faith and determinacion of holy churche I have bothe secretly and openly holden, beleved, affermed and taught. And specially among all other things, thies errours and heresies folowing, that is to witte.

First, that the blissed sacrament of the aulter ys not Crists very body but oonly materiall brede.

With other divers opinions contrary to the faith of Crist and determinacion of his churche aforsaid.

---

[c] and *repeated as first word on fo. 165v.*   [d] Thomas Browne *in margin.*

Wherfore I, the forsaid Thomas Browne, willing hereaftir to beleve in the faith of Crist and of his churche and to folowe the true doctrine of holy churche, with a pure hert forsake and utterly despise my said errors, heresies and damnable opinions and confesse them to be contrarius and repugnaunt to the faith of Criste and determinacion of his holy churche. And therfore the said errors, heresies and opinions in especiall and all other errors and heresies, fals doctrynes and damned opinions in generall likewise contrary and repugnaunt to the faith of Criste and deteminacion of his churche aforsaid I abjure, forsake and utterly renownce here bifore yor gracious lordship and all the honorable audience here assembled. And over that I swere by thies holy evangelies by me bodily here touched that from hensforth I shall never holde, teche, bileve or afferme the forsaid heresies, errors and damnable opinions nor noon other ayenst the faith of Crists holy churche and determinacion of the same. Nor yet I shall by myself or any other persone privatly or apertly defende, maynteigne, socor, favor or support any persone that to my knowlege holdeth, beleveth, affermeth or techeth any suche error, heresie or damned opinions nor any persone yat is suspect of the same. And if I may knowe hereaftir any persone of suche error, heresie or of any suche fals doctryne or any opinions contrary to the comen doctrine of the churche aforsaid, or if I may knowe any of their fautors, comforters, concelors or defensors or any that have suspect books or quayers of suche errors, heresies and damned opinions, I shal without delay give knowlege unto yor goode lordship or to yor successors or to the ordinary or ordinaries of the same persones or elles unto yor and their officers. So God me helpe and holy dome and thies holy evangelies.

In wittnes wherof to thies presents with myn owne hand I have made and subscribed the signe of the holy crosse +

Their penances. Et tunc ibidem dominus iniunxit eisdem quod die Dominica ad septimanam et tribus diebus Dominicis ex tunc sequentibus, coram processione in ecclesiis suis parochialibus, portabit eorum uterque fasciculum ligneum. Et post processionem expectabunt ibidem in navi ecclesie usque post missam, gestantes huiusmodi fasciculum.

Item quod si noverint aliquos de heresi suspectos aut libros de heresi habentes, certificent eundem reverendissimum patrem indilate.

Item quod non amoveant se a parochiis ubi iam inhabitant, nisi habita licentia ab eodem reverendissimo patre aut suis successoribus.

Item quod eorum uterque gestabit fasciculum depictum super humero suo sinistro vestimenti sui superioris, nisi aliter fuerit secum dispensatum per dictum reverendissimum patrem aut suos successores.

Deinde idem reverendissimus pater dispensavit cum eisdem pro uno anno integro proxime futuro ab usu dicti fasciculi, ita quod in fine anni huiusmodi presentabunt se dicto reverendissimo patri aut suis successoribus ubicumque tunc fuerint.

19. ABJURATION AND PENANCE OF JOHN FRANKE OF TENTERDEN, 16 AUGUST, 1511 [fos. 165V–166R]

His appearance in court etc. Eisdem die et loco[1] coram eodem reverendissimo patre pro tribunali sedente, presentibus tunc ibidem magistris Willelmo Warham, archiepiscopo[a] Cantuariense, Cuthberto Tunstall, Thoma Welles, Gabriele Silvester, utriusque iuris et sacre pagine doctoribus, ac Thoma Milling et aliis, comparuit personaliter Johannes Franke de Tenterden. Qui tunc ibidem abiuravit omnes hereses et erroneas suas opiniones contra fidem catholicam et ecclesie universalis determinationem, secundum quod continetur in scedula sue abiurationis per eum publice recitata et manu sua propria crucis signo signata: prestito primitus per eundem de peragendo penitentiam sibi per dictum reverendissimum patrem in ea parte iniungendam, ad sancta Dei evangelia per eum corporaliter tacta, iuramento corporali. Cuius scedule tenor sequitur videlicet.

His abjuration. In[b] the name of God, Amen. Bifore you, the most reverend fader in God my lord William, archiebisshop of Caunterbury, I, John Franke of Tenderden of yor diocise of Caunterbury, of my pure hert and free will confesse and knowlege that I in tymes passed bifore this houre, that is to witte by the space of . . . [c] yeres and more, have beleved, thought, said, holden, affermed and taught of the sacraments of the church and of the articles of the faith otherwise than the holy churche of Rome and universall churche of God techeth, holdeth and observeth. And many and divers open and damned errors and heresies contrary to the true and catholike faith and determinacion of holy churche I have bothe secretly and openly holden, beleved, affermed and taught. And specially among all other, thies errors and heresies folowing, that is to witte.

First, that the blissed sacrament of the aulter is not Cristes very body but oonly materiall brede.

Also that pilgremages to holy and devoute places be not necessary nor meritorious for mannys soule, but that money and labor doon and spent therabout is all in vayn.

Also that worshipping of images of the holy crucifixe, of our blissed lady and of other seynts is not to be doon nor profitable for mannys soule.

Wherfore I, the forsaid John Franke, willing hereaftir to beleve in the faith of Criste and of his churche and to folowe the true doctrine of

---

[1] See above, 87.

[a] *MS.* arch'no.   [b] Johannes Franke *in margin.*   [c] *Blank space in MS.*

holy churche, with a pure hert forsake and utterly despise my said errors, heresies and damnable opinions and confesse them to be contrarious and repugnaunt to the faith of Criste and determinacion of his holy churche. And therfore the said errors, heresies and opinions in especiall and all other errors and heresies, fals doctrynes and damned opinions in generall lykewise contrary and repugnaunt to the faith of Criste and determinacion of his churche aforsaid I abjure, forsake and utterly renownce here bifore yor gracious lordship and all the honorabill audience here assembled. And over that I swere by thies holy evangelies by me bodily here touched that from hensforth I shall never hold, teche, beleve or afferme the forsaid heresies, errors and damnable opinions nor noon other ageynst the faith of Crists holy churche and determinacion of the same. Nor yet I shall by myself or any other persone privatly or apertly defende, mayn[fo. 166r]teyne, socor, favor or support any persone that to my knowlege holdeth, beleveth, affermeth or techeth any suche error, heresie or damned opinion nor any persone that is suspect of the same. And if I may know hereaftir any persone of suche error, heresie or of any suche fals doctrynes or any opinions contrary to the commen doctrine of the church aforesaid, or if I may knowe any of their fautors, confortors, concelors or defensors or any that have suspect books or quayers of suche errours, heresies and damned opinions, I shall without delay geve knowlege unto youre goode lordship or to your successors or to the ordinarie or ordinaries of the same persones or elles unto yor and their officers. So God me helpe and holy dome and thies holy evangelies.

In wittnes wherof to these presents with myn owne hand I have made and subscribed the signe of the holy crosse +

His penance. Et idem reverendissimus pater iniunxit eidem quod – nudus tibias, pedes et caput – antecedat in processione die nativitatis beate Marie virginis[2] proxime futuro, gestans cereum in manu sua, circa ecclesiam parochialem de Tenterden. Et tempore offertorii offeret eundem ad manum sacerdotis altam missam ibidem celebrantis.

Item quod non mutabit locum mansionis sue, nisi prius habita licentia a dicto reverendissimo patre aut suis successoribus.

---

[2] 8 September, feast of the birthday of St. Mary.

20. ABJURATIONS AND PENANCES OF JOYCE BAMPTON OF BEARSTED,
RICHARD BAMPTON OF BOXLEY, ROBERT BRIGHT OF MAIDSTONE AND
WILLIAM LORKYN OF EAST FARLEIGH, 3 SEPTEMBER, 1511 [fos. 166R–167R]

Their appearance in court etc. Tercio die mensis Septembris anno
Domini millesimo quingentesimo undecimo in capella manerii dicti
reverendissimi patris de Maidston, coram eodem reverendissimo patre
pro tribunali ut superius iudicialiter sedente, presentibus tunc ibidem
reverendissimo patre domino Johanne . . . [1] episcopo ac venerabilibus
viris magistris Cuthberto Tunstall, Gabriele Silvester, doctoribus
superius nominatis, priore de Leds,[2] magistro Thoma Milling et aliis,
comparuerunt personaliter Jocosa Bampton de Bersted, Ricardus
Bampton de Boxley, Robertus Bright de Maidston et Willelmus Lorkyn
de East Farley. Qui abiurarunt et eorum quilibet abiuravit omnes
hereses et erroneas suas opiniones contra fidem catholicam et ecclesie
universalis determinationem, secundum quod continetur in scedulis
suarum abiurationum per eos et eorum quemlibet publice recitatis et
manibus suis propriis crucis signo signatis: prestito primitus per
eosdem et eorum quemlibet de peragendo penitentian eis et eorum
cuilibet per dictum reverendissimum patrem in ea parte iniungendam,
ad sancta Dei evangelia per eorum singulos corporaliter tacta,
iuramento corporali. Quarum scedularum tenores sequuntur videlicet.

Abjuration of Joyce Bampton. In[a] the name of God, Amen. Bifore you,
the most reverend fader in God my lord William archiebisshop of
Caunterbury, I, Joyce Bampton the wif of John Bampton of Bersted of
yor diocise of Caunterbury, of my pure hert and free will confesse and
knowlege that I in diverse tymes passed bifore this houre, that is to
witte by the space of vii yeres and more, have beleved, thought, saide,
holden, affermed and taught of the sacraments of the churche and of the
articles of the faith otherwise than the holy church of Rome and
universall churche of God techeth, holdeth and observeth. And many
and divers open and damned errors and heresies contrary to the true and
catholike faith and deteminacion of holy churche I have bothe secretly
and openly holden, bileved, affermed and taught. And specially among
all other, thies errors and heresies folowing, that is to witte:

First, that the blissed sacrament of the aulter is not Crists verey body
but oonly materiall brede.

And that pilgremages to holy and devoute places be not necessary

---

[1] Blank space in MS. John Thornden may be intended (see above, 4, note 8).
[2] See above, 56, note 8.

[a] Jocosa Bampton *in margin.*

nor meritorious for mannys soule, but that money and labor doon and spent theraboute is all in vayne.

Also that worshipping of images of the holy crucifixe, of our blissed Lady and of other seynts is not to be doon nor profitable for mannys soule.

Wherfore I, the forsaid Joyce Bampton, willing hereaftir to beleve in the faith of Crist and to folowe the true doctrine of holy church, with a pure hert forsake and utterly despise my said errors, heresies and damnable opinions and confesse theym to be contrarius and repugnaunt to the faith of Crist and determinacion of his holy church. And therfore the said errors, heresies and opinions in especiall and all other errors and heresies, fals doctrines and damned opinions in generall likewise contrary and repugnaunt to the faith of Criste and determinacion of his churche aforsaid I abjure, forsake and utterly renownce here bifore yor gracious lordship and all the honorable audience here assembled. And over that I swere by thies holy evangelies by me bodily here touched that from hensforth I shall never hold, teche, beleve or afferme the forsaid heresies, errors and damnable opinions nor noon other ayenst the faith of Crists holy churche and determinacion of the same. Nor yet I shall by myself or any other persone pryvatly or apertly defende, maynteyne, socor, favor or support any persone that to my knowlege holdeth, beleveth, affermeth or techeth any suche error, heresie or damned opinion nor any persone that is suspect of the same. And if I may knowe hereaftir any persone of suche error, heresie or of any suche fals doctrynes or any opinions contrary to the commen doctrine of the churche aforsaid, or if I may knowe any of their fautors, comfortors, concelours or defensors or any that have suspect books or quayers of suche errors, heresies and damned opinions, I shall without delay geve knowlege unto yor good lordship and to yor successors or to the ordinarye or ordinaries of the same persones or elles unto yor and their officers. So God me helpe and holy dome and thies holy evangelies.

In wittnes wherof to these presents with myn owne hand I have made and subscribed the signe of the holy crosse. Jocosa Bampton +

Abjuration of Richard Bampton. In[b] the name of God, Amen. Bifore you, the moost reverend fader in God my lord William, archiebishop of Caunterbury, I, Richard Bampton, of my pure hert and free will con-fesse and knowlege that I in tymes passed bifore this houre, that is to witte by the space of . . . [c] yeres and more, have beleved, thought, said, holden, affermed and taught of the sacraments of the churche and of the

---

[b] Ricardus Bampton de Boxley *in margin.*   [c] *Blank space in MS.*

articles of the faith otherwise than the holy churche of Rome and universall churche of God techeth, holdeth and observeth. And many and divers open and damned errors and heresies contrary to the true and catholik faith and determinacion of holy churche I have bothe secretly and openly holden, beleved, affermed and taught. And specially among all other, thies errors and heresies folowing, that is to witte.

First, that the blissed sacrament of the aulter ys not Crists verey body but oonly materiall brede.

Also that pilgremages to holy and devoute places be not necessary nor meritorious for mannys soule, but yat money and labor doon and spent thereabout is all in vayn.

Also that worshipping of ymages of the holy crucifixe, of our blissed Lady and of other seynts is not to be doon nor profitable for mannys soule.

Wherfore I, the forsaid Richard Bampton, willing hereaftir to bileve in the faithe of Criste and of his churche and to folowe the true doctrine of holy churche, with a pure hert forsake and utterly despise my said errors, heresies and damnable opinions and confesse theym to be contrarious and repugnaunt to the faith of Crist and determinacion of his holy churche. And therfore the said errors, heresies and opinions in especiall and all other errors and heresies, fals doctrines and damned opinions in generall likewise contrary and repugnaunt to the faith of Crist and determinacion of his church aforesaid I abjure, forsake and utterly renownce here bifore yor gracious lordship and all the honorable audience [fo. 166v] here assembled. And over that I swere by thies holy evangelies by me bodily touched that from hensforth I shall never holde or teche, beleve or afferme the forsaid heresies, errors and damnable opinions nor noon other ayenst the faith of Cristes holy churche and determinacion of the same. Nor yet I shall by myself or any other persone pryvatly or apertly defende, maynteyne, socor, favor or support any persone that to my knowlege holdeth, beleveth, affermeth or techeth any suche error, heresie or damned opinion nor any persone that ys suspect of the same. And if I may knowe hereaftir any persone of suche error, heresie or of any suche false doctrynes or any opinions contrary to the commen doctryne of the church aforsaid, or if I may know any of their fautors, comfortors, concelors or defensours or any that have suspect books or quayers of suche errours, heresies and damned opinions, I shall without delay geve knowlege unto yor good lordship or to yor successors or to the ordinarie or ordinaries of the same persones or elles unto yor and their officers. So God me helpe and holy dome and thies holy evangelies.

In wittnes wherof to thies presents with myn owne hand I have made and subscribed the signe of the holy crosse. Ricardus Bampton +

Abjuration of Robert Bright. In[d] the name of God, Amen. Bifore you, the most reverend fader in God my lord William archiebisshop of Caunterbury, I, Robert Bright of Maidston of your diocise of Caunterbury, of my pure hert and free will confesse and knowlege that I in tymes passed bifore this houre, that is to witte by the space of xiiii yeres and more have beleved, thought, said, holden, affermed and taught of the sacraments of the church and of the articles of the faith otherwise than the holy churche of Rome and universall churche of God techeth, holdeth and observeth. And many and diverse open and damned errors and heresies contrary to the true and catholik faith and determinacion of holy churche I have bothe secretly and opynly holden, beleved, affermed and taught. And specially among all other, thies errors and heresies folowing, that is to witte.

First, that the blissed sacrament of the aulter ys not Crists verey body but oonly materiall brede.

Also that pilgremages to holy and devoute places be not necessary nor meritorious for mannys soule, but that money and labour doon and spent thereaboute ys all in vayne.

Also that worshipping of ymages of the holy crucifixe, of our blissed Lady and of other saynts is not to be doon nor profittable for mannys soule.

Also that holy bredde and holy water be not the better aftir the benediccion made by the prest than it was bifore the benediccion.

Wherfore I, the forsaid Robert Bright, willing hereaftir to beleve in the faith of Criste and of his church and to folowe the true doctrine of holy churche, with a pure hert forsake and utterly despise my said errors, heresies and damnable opinions and confesse theym to be contrarius and repugnaunt to the faith of Criste and determinacion of his holy churche. And therfore the saide errors, heresies and opinions in especiall and all other errors and heresies, fals doctrines and damned opinions in generall likewise contrary and repugnaunt to the faith of Criste and determinacion of his churche forsaid I abjure, forsake and utterly renownce here bifore your gracious lordship and all the honorable audience here assembled. And over that I swere by thies holy evangelies by me bodily here touched that from hensforth I shall never holde, teche, beleve or afferme the forsaid heresies, errors and damnable opinions nor noon other ayenst the faith of Crists holy churche and determinacion of the same. Nor yet I shall be meself or any other persone privatly or apertly defende, maynteyne, socor, favor or support any persone that to my knowlege holdeth, beleveth, affermeth or techeth any suche error, heresie or damned opinion nor

---

[d] Robertus Bright *in margin.*

any persone that is suspect of the same. And if I may know hereaftir any persone of suche error, heresie or of any suche false doctrynes or any opinions contrary to the commen doctryne of the churche aforsaid, or if I may know any of their fautors, comfortors, concelors or defensors or any that have suspect books or quayers of suche errors, heresies and damned opinions, I shall without delay geve knowlege unto yor goode lordship or to yor successors or to the ordinarie or ordinaries of the same persones or elles unto yor and their officers. Soo God me helpe and holy dome and thies holy evaungelies.

In wittnes wherof to these presents with myn owne hand I have made and subscribed the signe of the holy crosse. Robertus Bright +

Abjuration of William Lorkyn. In[e] the name of God, Amen. Bifore you, the moost reverend fader in God my lord William archebisshop of Caunterbury, I, William Lorkyn of the parisshe of East Farley of yor diocise of Caunterbury, of my pure hert and free will confesse and knowlege yat I in tymes passed bifore this howre, that is to witte by the space of . . . [f] yeres and more, have beleved, thought, said, holden, affermed and taught of the sacraments of the churche and of the articles of the faith otherwise than the holy church of Rome and universall churche of God techeth, holdeth and observeth. And many divers open and damned errors and heresies contrary to the true and catholik faith and determinacion of holy churche I have bothe secretly and openly holden, beleved, affermed and taught. And specially among all other, thies errors and heresies folowing, that is to witte.

First, that the sacrament of the aulter is not Crists verey body but oonly materiall bred.

Also that pilgremages to holy and devoute places be not necessary nor meritorius for mannys soule, but that money and labor doon and spent thereabout is all in vayne.

Also that worshipping of images of the holy crucifixe, of our blissed Lady and of other seynts is not to be doon nor profitable for mannys soule.

Wherfore I, the forsaid William Lorkyn, willing hereaftir to beleve in the faith of Crist and of his church and to folowe the true doctrine of holy churche, with a pure hert forsake and utterly despise my said errors, heresies and damnable opinions and confesse theym to be contrarius and repugnaunt to the faith of Crist and determinacion of his holy church. And therfore the said errors, heresies and opinions in especiall and all other errors and heresies, fals doctrines and damned opinions in generall likewise contrary and repugnaunt to the faith of

---

[e] Willelmus Lorkyn *in margin.*   [f] *Blank space in MS.*

Criste and determinacion of his churche aforsaid I abjure, forsake and utterly renownce here bifore yor gracious lordship and all the honorable audience here assembled. And over that I swere by thies holy evangelies by me here bodily touched that from hensforth I shall never holde, teche, beleve or afferme the aforsaid errors, heresies and damnable opinions nor noon other ayenst the faith of Crists holy church and determinacion of the same. Nor yet I shall by myself or any other persone privatly or apertly defende, maynteyne, socor, favor or support any persone that to my knowlege holdeth, beleveth, affermeth or techeth any suche error, heresie or damned opinion nor any persone that is suspect of the same. And if I may know hereaftir any persone of suche error, heresie or of any suche fals doctrines or any opinions contrary to the commen doctrine of ye churche aforsaid, or if I may know any of their fautors, comfortors, concelors or defensors or any that have suspect books or quayers of suche errors, heresies or damned opinions, I shall without delay geve knowlege unto yor good lordship and to yor successors or to the ordinary or ordinaries of the same persones or elles unto yor and their officers. So God me helpe and holy dome and these holy evangelies.

In wittnes wherof to these presents with myn owne hand I have made and subscribed the signe of the holy crosse. William Lorkyn +

Their penances. Et tunc ibidem idem reverendissimus pater iniunxit eisdem, videlicet Jocose Bampton et Ricardo Bampton quod duabus Dominicis proxime futuris, ac Roberto Bright et Willelmo Lorkyn tribus diebus Dominicis proxime futuris,[g] [fo. 167r] in ecclesiis suis parochialibus gestabunt, et eorum quilibet gestabit, ante processionem fasciculum ligneum. Et post processionem eorum quilibet stabit, gestans huiusmodi fasciculum in medio ecclesie, quousque missa finiatur.

Item quod si noverint aliquos suspectos de heresi aut libros de heresi habentes, quod certificabunt dictum reverendissimus patrem aut suos successores etc.

Item quod si se amoverint a parochiis ubi nunc inhabitant, morandi causa, quod reddant dictum reverendissimum patrem aut suos successores de locis quos inhabitare proposuerint certiores.

Item prefato Roberto Bright quod qualibet die Dominica durante vita sua dicat in ecclesia sua parochiali quinque Pater noster, quinque Ave Maria et unum Credo.

[g] in ecclesiis *at foot of page.*

21. PENANCE OF JOHN GREBILL[1] OF BENENDEN, 3 SEPTEMBER, 1511
[fo. 168V]

His appearance in court etc. Tercio die mensis Septembris anno Domini millesimo quingentesimo undecimo in capella manerii prefati reverendissimi patris etc. de Maidston, coram eodem reverendissimo patre pro tribunali tunc ibidem iudicialiter sedente, presentibus tunc ibidem reverendo patre . . . [a] episcopo, eidem reverendissimo patri assidente,[b] magistris Cuthberto Tunstall, domino priore de Ledys,[2] Gabriele Silvester, sacre theologie professore, Thoma Milling, et aliis, comparuit personaliter Johannes Grebill. Contra quem idem reverendissimus pater perpetuis carceribus mancipandum fore decrevit et mancipavit, videlicet in prioratu de Bilsington[3] Cantuariensis diocesis. Et monuit eundem sub pena relapsus quod non recedat a sceptis dicti prioratus ultra unum miliare sine licencia dicti reverendissimi patris aut successorum suorum durante vita sua. Et tunc ibidem iniunxit eidem quod quolibet[c] die Veneris durante vita sua abstinebit in pane et aqua, nisi aliter fuerit secum dispensatum per eundem reverendissimus patrem, ut prefertur, aut suos successores; et quod intrabit dictum prioratum infra quindecim dies immediate futuros. Cuius sententie tenor sequitur videlicet.

Sentence. In[d] Dei nomine, Amen. Nos, Willelmus permissione divina Cantuariensis archiepiscopus, totius Anglie primas et apostolice sedis legatus, in quodam negocio heretice pravitatis contra te, Johannem Grebill de Benynden nostre Cantuariensis diocesis ac nostre iurisdictioni notorie subditum et subiectum, coram nobis in iudicio personaliter comparentem, ex officio nostro mero, rite et canonice procedentes – auditis et intellectis, visis, cognitis rimatisque ac matura deliberatione discussis et ponderatis dicti negocii meritis, servatisque in omnibus et per omnia in eodem negocio de iure servandis ac quomodolibet requisitis – pro tribunali sedentes et solum Deum pre oculis nostris habentes.

Quia per acta, actitata, deducta et probata coram nobis in negocio antedicto et per te confessata, recognita et exhibita etiam coram nobis in

---

[1] He is described below as 'of Benenden' and elsewhere John Grebill senior is referred to thus, though sometimes as 'of Tenterden'; whereas his son, John Grebill junior, is described invariably as 'of Tenterdon'. There is the fact, too, that the father appears to have been far more heavily involved in Lollardy than his son, so that he is much more likely to have been the subject of the severe sentence involved here, perpetual imprisonment. So, it seems clear that the person in question here is the father, John Grebill senior.

[2] See above, 56, note 8.

[3] The priory of Augustinian canons at Bilsington, Kent.

---

[a] *Blank space in MS.*　　[b] presentibus *repeated.*　　[c] *MS.* qualibet.

[d] Sententia contra Johannem Grebill *in margin.*

eodem, invenimus te per tuam confessionem ac alias probationes legitimas coram nobis iudicialiter factas nonnullos et varios errores, hereses et damnatas opiniones iuri divino et ecclesiastico obviantes, contrarios et repugnantes contra fidem orthodoxam determinatam et observatam per universalem catholicam et apostolicam ecclesiam tenuisse, credidisse, asseruisse, affirmasse et dogmatisasse: ac alios quamplures Christi fideles perversa et insana doctrina tua heretice pravitatis labe infecisse: ac eos huiusmodi errores, hereses et damnatas opiniones contra fidem orthodoxam et determinationem sacrosancte Romane et universalis ecclesie assidue et accurate docuisse: eosdem a fidei catholice et sancte matris ecclesie unitate avertendo et segregando ac quantum in te fuit avertisse et segregasse. Nunc tamen saniori usus consilio vis ad unitatem ecclesie, prout asseris, de corde puro et bono et fide non ficta redire.

Idcirco, de consilio iurisperitorum cum quibus communicavimus in hac parte – abiurata per te primitus omni heretica pravitate secundum formam eccclesie consuetam, ac prestita cautione de parendo iuri et stando mandatis ecclesie ac iniunctionibus nostris tibi occasione premissorum factis et faciendis, et de fideliter perimplendo penitentiam per nos tibi in hac parte assignatam et assignandam – ab excommunicationis sententia, quam ea occasione incurristi, te absolvimus et sacramentis ecclesie et communioni fidelium restituimus. In nomine Patris et Filii et Spiritus sancti.

Et quia in Deum omnipotentem et sanctam ecclesiam catholicam predictis modis temere deliquisti ac etiam indoles innocentes et alios Christicolas quamplures perversa et insana doctrina tua heretice pravitatis labe infecisti, ne gregem dominicum in futurum heretice pravitatis contagio de quo plurimum timemus inficias, peractis primitus per te aliis iniunctionibus et penitenciis tibi a nobis iudicialter modo assignatis et assignandis, te in prioratum canonicorum de Bilsington nostre Cantuariensis diocesis ad perpetuam illic agendam penitenciam detrudendum esse adiudicamus et decernimus. Ita quod a dicto prioratu de Bilsington ultra spacium unius miliaris non exeas^e aut recedas, sed illic vita tua durante pane doloris et aqua angustie sustentandum esse volumus, decernimus et mandamus per hanc nostram sententiam diffinitivam, quam promulgamus et ferimus in hiis scriptis. Reservata nobis et successoribus nostris Cantuariensibus archiepiscopis dumtaxat potestate penam sive penitenciam supradictam, si nobis aut successoribus nostris huiusmodi iustum visum fuerit, mitigandi seu alias commutandi.

Commutation. Deinde idem reverendissimus pater commutavit penitentiam dicti Johannis Grebill, quoad abstinenciam in pane et aqua, in abstinentiam ab usu camisie linee quarta et sexta feria cuiuslibet ebdomada durante vita sua, sic quod ipse Johannes dum vixerit quarta et sexta feria cuiuslibet ebdomade huiusmodi non utatur camisia linea.

---

^e *MS.* exies.

22. ABJURATION AND PENANCE OF JOHN BAUS[1] OF BOXLEY, 4 SEPTEMBER, 1511 [fo. 167R]

His appearance in court etc. Quarto die mensis Septembris anno Domini supradicto in ecclesia collegiata de Maidston[2] predict', coram eodem reverendissimo patre pro tribunali ut superius iudicialiter sedente, assidente eidem reverendo patre . . . [a] episcopo, presentibus venerabilibus viris magistris Cuthberto Tunstall, Clemente Browne, Thoma Welles, superius nominatis, et pluribus aliis, comparuit personaliter Johannes Baus de Boxley. Et tunc ibidem in forma superius expressa [. . .], iuxta contenta in scedula sue abiurationis per eum de verbo ad verbum recitata, quam scedulam signo crucis manu sua propria signavit: prestito primitus per eundem iuramento corporali de peragendo penitenciam in ea parte iniungendam sibi per dictum reverendissimum patrem, ad sancta Dei evangelia per eum corporaliter tacta. Cuius scedule tenor sequitur videlicet.

His abjuration. In[b] the name of God, Amen. Bifore you, the most reverend fader in God my lord William, archiebisshop of Caunterbury, I, John Baus of the parisshe of Boxley of yor diocise of Caunterbury, of my pure hert and free will confesse and knowlege that [I] in tymes passed bifore this houre, that is to witte by the space of xvi yeres and more, have beleved, thought, said, holden, affermed and taught[c] of the sacraments of the churche and of the articles of the faith otherwise than the holy churche of Rome and universall churche of God techeth, holdeth and observeth. And many and diverse open and damned errors and heresies contrary to the true and catholik faith and determynacion of holy churche I have bothe secretly and openly holden, beleved, affermed and taught. And specially among all other, thies errors and heresies folowing, that is to witte.

First, that the blissed sacrament of the aulter is not Crists verey body but oonly materiall bredde.

Also that pilgremages to holy and divers[d] places be not necessary nor meritorious for mannys soule, but that money and labor doon and spent thereabout ys all in vayne.

Also that worshipping of images of the holy crucifixe, of our blissed Lady and other seynts is not to be doon nor profitable for mannys soule.

[1] It is impossible to know whether his name was 'Baus' or 'Bans', since 'u' and 'n' are indistinguishable.
[2] The collegiate church of All Saints in Maidstone.

[a] *Blank space in MS.*   [b] Johannes Baus *in margin.*   [c] *MS.* thaught.   [d] divers *sic.*

Also that confession made to a preest is not necessary for mannys soule.

Wherfore I, the forsaid John Baus, willing hereaftir to beleve in the faith of Crist and of his churche and to folowe the true doctryne of holy church, with a pure hert forsake and utterly despise my said errors, heresies and damnable opinions and confesse theym to be contrarious and repugnaunt to the faith of Crist and determinacion of his holy churche.

And therfore the said errors, heresies and damned opinions in especiall and all other errours and heresies, fals doctrines and damned opinions in generall likewise contrary and repugnaunt to the faith of Crist and determinacion of his churche aforsaid I abjure, forsake and utterly renownce here bifore yor gracious lordship and all the honorable audience here assembled. And over that I swere by thies holy evaungelies by me bodily here touched that from hensforth I shall never holde, teche, beleve or afferme the forsaid heresies, errors and damnable opinions nor noon other ayenst the faith of Crists holy churche and determinacion of the same. Nor yet I shall by myself nor any other persone pryvatly or apertly defende, maynteyn, socor, favor or support any persone that to my knowlege holdeth, beleveth, affermeth or techeth any suche error, heresie or damned opinion nor any persone that ys suspect of the same. And if I may know hereaftur any persone of suche error, heresie or of any suche fals doctrines or any opinions contrary to the commen doctrine of the churche aforsaid, or if I may knowe any of their fautors, comfortors, concelors or defensors or any that have suspect books or quayers of suche errors, heresies or damned opinions, I shall withoute delaye geve knowlege unto yor good lordship or to yor successors or to the ordinarie or ordinaries of the same persones or elles unto yor and their officers. So God me helpe and holi doom and thies holy evaungelies.

In wittnes wherof to these presents with myn owne hand I have made and subscribed the signe of the holy crosse. + Joh'es Baus of the parisshe of Boxley

His penance. Et insuper tunc ibidem idem reverendissimus pater iniunxit eidem Johanni Baus quod die Dominica proxime et immediate futura in ecclesia parochiali de Boxley sedebit in medio eiusdem ecclesie parochialis, gestans fasciculum ligneum, quousque magna missa finiatur ibidem ipso die. Et quod prius ipso die in eadem ecclesia antecedat processionem, gestans huiusmodi fasciculum. Et quod die Dominica proxima similem peraget penitentian in eadem ecclesia.

Item quod si aliquos noverit de heresi suspectos sive libros de heresi habentes, revelabit eidem reverendissimo patri aut suis successoribus.

Item quod si se amoverit ad alium locum, morandi causa, reddat dictum reverendissimum patrem indilate aut suos successores inde certiores.

23. ABJURATION AND PENANCE OF JOAN LOWES OF CRANBROOK, 4 SEPTEMBER, 1511 [fos. 167*V–168R]

Her appearance in court etc. Quarto die Septembris anno Domini mill-esimo quingentesimo undecimo in ecclesia collegiata de Maidston[1] predicta, coram prefato reverendissimo patre pro tribunali iudicialiter sedente, assidente eidem reverendo patre . . . [a] episcopo, presentibus magistris Cuthberto Tunstall, Clemente Browne, Thoma Welles, doctoribus, et pluribus aliis, comparuit personaliter Johanna Lowes de Cranebroke. Et tunc ibidem abiuravit omnes hereses et errores, iuxta contenta in scedula abiurationis sue per eam publice recitata de verbo ad verbum, quam scedulam sua manu signavit signo crucis: prestito primitus per eandem de peragendo penitentiam sibi per dictum reverendissimum patrem in ea parte iniungendam, ad sancta Dei evangelia per eam corporaliter tacta, iuramento corporali. Cuius scedule tenor sequitur videlicet.

Her abjuration. In[b] the name of God, Amen. Bifore you, the most reverend fader in God my lord William archibisshop of Caunterbury, I, Johanne Lowes the wif of Thomas Lowes of yor diocise of Caunterbury, of my pure hert and free will confesse and knowlege that I in tymes passid bifore this houre, that is to witte by the space of . . . [c] yeres and more, have beleved, thought, said, holden, affermed and taught of the sacraments of the churche and of the articles of the faith otherwise than the holy church of Rome and universall churche of God techeth, holdeth and observeth. And many and divers open and damned errors and heresies contrary to the true and catholike faith and determinacion of holy churche I have bothe secretly and openly holden, beleved, affermed and taught. And specially among all other, thies errors and heresies folowing, that is to witte.

First, that the blissed sacrament of the aulter is not Crists verey body but oonly materiall brede.

Also that pilgremages to holy and devoute places be not necessary nor meritorius for mannys soule, but that money and labor doon and spent thereaboute is all in vayne.

Also that worshipping of ymages of the holy crucifixe, of our blissed Lady and of other seynts is not to be doon nor profitable for mannys soule.

Wherfore I, the forsaid Johanne Lowes, willing hereaftir to beleve in the faith of Criste and of his churche and to folowe the true doctrine of

---

[1] See above, 100, note 2.

[a] *Blank space in MS.*   [b] Johanna Lowes *in margin.*   [c] *Blank space in MS.*

holy churche, with a pure hert forsake and utterly despise my said errors, heresies and damnable opinions and confesse them to be contrarius and repugnaunt to the faith of Criste and determinacion of his holy churche. And therfore the said errors, heresies and opinions in especiall and all other errors and heresies, fals doctrines and damned opinions in generall likewise contrary and repugnaunt to the faith of Criste and determinacion of his churche aforsaid I abjure, forsake and utterly renownce here bifore yor gracious lordship and all the honorable audience here assembled. And over that I swere by thies holy evangelies by me bodily here touched that from hensforth I shall never holde, teche, beleve or afferme the forsaid errors, heresies and damnable opinions nor noon other ayenst the faith of Crists holy churche and determinacion of the same. Nor yet I shall by myself or any other persone pryvatly or apertly defende, maynteyne, socor, favor or support any persone that to my knowlege holdeth, beleveth, affermeth or techeth any suche error, heresie or damned opinion nor any persone that is suspect of the same. And if I may knowe hereaftir any persone of suche error, heresie or of any suche fals doctrines or any opinions contrary to the commen doctryne of the churche aforsaid, or if I may know any of their fautors, comfortors, concelours or defensors or any that have suspect books or quayers of suche errors, heresies or damned opinions, I shall withoute delay geve knowlege unto yor good lordship or to yor successors or to the ordinary or ordinaries of the same persones or elles unto yor and their officers. So God me helpe and holy dome and thies holy evangelies.

In wittnes wherof to thies presents with myn owne hand I have made and subscribed the signe of the holy crosse. + Johanna Lowes, uxor Thome Lowes de Cranebroke.

Her penance. Et deinde idem reverendissimus pater tulit sententiam contra eandem in scriptis, eo quod defecit in purgatione sua. Per quam eandem perpetuis carceribus mancipavit, videlicet in monasterio monialium de Shepeya,[2] ita quod non recedat a dicto monasterio ultra spacium unius miliaris durante vita sua. Et monuit eandem quod intrabit dictum monasterium citra quartum diem Octobris proxime futurum. Cuius sentencie tenor sequitur.

Sentence. In[d] Dei nomine, Amen. Nos, Willelmus permissione divina Cantuariensis archiepiscopus, totius Anglie primas et apostolice sedis

---

[2] The priory of Augustinian nuns at Minster, Isle of Sheppey.

[d] Sententia contra dictam Johannam *in margin.*

legatus, in quodam negocio heretice pravitatis contra te, Johannam
Lowes, uxorem Thome Lowes de Cranebroke nostre Cantuariensis
diocesis ac nostre jurisdictioni notorie subditam et subiectam, coram
nobis in iudicio personaliter comparentem, ex officio nostro mero, rite
et canonice procedentes – auditis et intellectis, visis, cognitis rimatisque ac matura deliberatione discussis et ponderatis dicti negocii
meritis, servatisque in omnibus et per omnia in eodem negocio de iure
servandis ac quomodolibet requisitis – pro tribunali sedentes et solum
Deum pre oculis nostris habentes.

Quia per acta, actitata, deducta et probata coram nobis in negocio
antedicto et per te confessata, recognita et exhibita etiam coram nobis
in eodem, invenimus te per tuam confessionem ac alias probationes
legitimas coram nobis iudicialiter factas nonnullos et varios errores,
hereses et damnatas opiniones iuri divino et ecclesiastico obviantes,
contrarios et repugnantes contra fidem orthodoxam determinatam et
observatam per universalem catholicam et apostolicam ecclesiam
tenuisse, credidisse, asseruisse, affirmasse et dogmatisasse: ac alios
quamplures Christi fideles perversa et insana doctrina tua heretice
pravitatis labe infecisse: ac eos huiusmodi errores, hereses et damnatas
opiniones contra fidem orthodoxam et determinationem sacrosancte
Romane et universalis ecclesie assidue et accurate docuisse: eosdem a
fidei catholice et sancte matris ecclesie unitate avertando et segregando
ac quantum in te fuit avertisse et segregasse. Nunc vero saniori usa
consilio vis ad unitatem ecclesie, prout asseris, de corde puro et bono et
fide non ficta redire.

Idcirco, de consilio iurisperitorum cum quibus communicavimus in
hac parte – abiurata per te primitus omni heretica pravitate secundum
formam ecclesie consuetam ac prestita cautione de parendo iuri et
stando mandatis ecclesie ac iniunctionibus nostris tibi occasione
premissorum factis et faciendis et de fideliter perimplendo penitenciam
per nos tibi in hac parte assignatam et assignandam – ab excommunicationis sententiam, quam ea occasione incurristi, te absolvimus et
sacramentis ecclesie et communioni fidelium restituimus. In nomine
Patris et Filii et Spiritus sancti.

Et quia Deum omnipotentem et sanctam ecclesiam catholicam
predictis modis deliquisti ac etiam indoles innocentes et alios Christicolas quamplures perversa et insana doctrina tua heretice pravitatis labe
infecisti, ne gregem dominicum in futurum heretice pravitatis labe et
contagio de quo plurimum timemus inficias, peractis primitus per te
aliis iniunctionibus et penitenciis tibi a nobis iudicialiter modo
assignatis et assignandis, te in monasterio monialium de Shepeay nostre
Cantuariensis diocesis ad perpetuam illic agendam penitentiam
detrudendam esse adiudicamus et decernimus. Ita quod a dicto
monasterio monialium de Shepeay ultra spacium unius miliaris non

exiges aut recedas, sed illic vita tua durante pane doloris et aqua angustie sust[ent]endam esse volumus, decernimus et mandamus per hanc nostram sententiam diffinitivam, quam promulgamus et ferimus in his scriptis. Reservata nobis et successoribus nostris Cantuariensibus archiepiscopis dumtaxat potestate penam sive penitenciam supradictam, si nobis aut successoribus nostris hiuusmodi iustum visum fuerit, mitigandi seu alias commutandi.

Additional penance. Et insuper iniunxit eidem quod non utatur veste linea, Anglice a smokke, aliquo die Veneris durante [fo. 168r] vita sua, nisi aliquod festum principale contingat ipso die et nisi aliter fuerit secum dispensatum per dictum reverendissimum patrem aut suos successores.

24. PENANCE OF STEPHEN CASTELYN OF TENTERDEN, 11 SEPTEMBER, 1511
[fo. 168R]

His appearance in court etc. Undecimo die mensis Septembris anno
Domini millesimo quingentesimo undecimo, in quadam capella ex
parte occidentali chori ecclesie metropolitice Cantuariensis,[1] coram
prefato reverendissimo patre et domino, domino Willelmo Cantuariense
archiepiscopo etc., presentibus tunc ibidem venerabilibus viris magistris Cuthberto Tunstall, Clemente Browne et Gabriele Silvester,
superius nominatis, Willelmo Potkyn et David Cooper, notariis
publicis, et aliis, comparuit personaliter Stephanus Castelyn de
Tenterden, cutler. Contra quem idem reverendissimus pater tulit
sententiam in scriptis. Per quam eundem Stephanum perpetuis
carceribus mancipandum fore decrevit et pronunciavit, videlicet in
monasterio de Ledys,[2] iniungendum eidem sub pena relapsus quod non
recedat a sceptis dicti monasterii ultra spacium unius miliaris,[a] et quod
intret in dictum monasterium infra quindecim dies proxime futurum; et
insuper quod gestabit fasciculum ligneum ante processionem in
ecclesia parochiale de Tenterden more penitentis die Dominica proxime
futura etc. Cuius sentencie tenor sequitur videlicet.

Sentence. In[b] Dei nomine, Amen. Nos, Willelmus permissione divina
Cantuariensis archiepiscopus, totius Anglie primas et apostolice sedis
legatus, in quodam negocio heretice pravitatis contra te, Stephanum
Castlyn de Tenterden nostre Cantuariensis diocesis ac nostre iurisdictioni notorie subditum et subiectum, coram nobis in iudicio personaliter
comparentem, ex officio nostro mero, rite et canonice procedentes –
auditis et intellectus, visis, cognitis rimatisque ac matura deliberatione
discussis et ponderatis dicti negocii meritis, servatisque in omnibus et
per omnia in eodem negocio de iure servandis ac quomodolibet
requisitis – pro tribunali sedentes ac solum Deum pre oculis nostris
habentes.

Quia per acta, actitata, deducta et probata coram nobis in negocio
antedicto et per te confessata, recognita et exhibita etiam coram nobis
in negocio antedicto, invenimus te et per tuam confessionem et alias
probationes legitimas coram nobis iudicialiter factas nonnullos et
varios errores, hereses et damnatas opiniones iuri divino et ecclesiastico obviantes, contrarios et repugnantes contra fidem orthodoxam
determinatam et observatam per universalem catholicam et apostolicam

---

[1] Canterbury Cathedral.
[2] The priory of Augustinian canons at Leeds, Kent.

---

[a] sub pena relapsus *repeated.*   [b] Sententia contra Stephanum Castlyn *in margin.*

ecclesiam tenuisse, credidisse, asseruisse, affirmasse et dogmatisasse: ac alios quamplures Christi fideles perversa et insana doctrina tua heretice pravitatis labe infecisse: ac eos huiusmodi errores, hereses et damnatas opiniones contra fidem orthodoxam et determinationem sacrosancte Romane et universalis ecclesie assidue et accurate docuisse: eosdem a fidei catholice et sancte matris ecclesie unitate avertendo et segregando ac quantum in te fuit avertisse et segregasse. Nunc tamen saniori usus consilio vis ad unitatem ecclesie, prout asseris, de corde puro et bono et fide non ficta redire.

Idcirco, de consilio iurisperitorum cum quibus communicavimus in hac parte – abiurata per te primitus omni heretica pravitate secundum formam ecclesie consuetam, ac prestita cautione de parendo iuri et stando mandatis ecclesie [ac] iniunctionibus nostris tibi occasione premissorum factis et faciendis, et de fideliter perimplendo penitenciam per nos tibi in hac parte assignatam et assignandam – ab excommunicationis sententia, quam ea occasione incurristi, te absolvimus et sacramentis ecclesie et communioni fidelium restituimus. In nomine Patris et Filii et Spiritus sancti.

Et quia in Deum omnipotentem et sanctam ecclesiam catholicam predictis modis temere deliquisti ac etiam indoles innocentes ac alios Christicolas quamplures perversa et insana doctrina tua heretice pravitatis labe infecisti, ne gregem dominicum in futurum heretice pravitatis contagio de quo plurimum timemus inficias, peractis primitus per te aliis iniunctionibus et penitenciis tibi a nobis iudicialiter assignatis et assignandis, te in prioratum sancti Nicholai de Ledys nostre Cantuariensis diocesis ad perpetuam illic agendam penitenciam detrudendum esse adiudicamus et decernimus. Ita quod a dicto prioratu ultra spatium unius miliaris non exeas[c] aut recedas, sed illic vita tua durante pane doloris et aqua angustie sustentandum esse volumus, decernimus et mandamus per hanc nostram sententiam diffinitivam, quam promulgamus et ferimus in his scriptis. Reservata nobis et successoribus nostris Cantuariensibus archiepiscopis dumtaxat potestate penam sive penitenciam supradictam, si nobis aut successoribus nostris huiusmodi iustum visum fuerit, mitiganti seu alias commutandi.

[c] *MS.* exies.

107

25. ABJURATION AND PENANCE OF JULIAN HILLES OF TENTERDEN,
13 SEPTEMBER, 1511 [fo. 168R-V]

Her appearance in court etc. Terciodecimo die mensis Septembris anno
Domini quo supra, in quadam capella sive oratorio infra palatium
reverendissimi patris antedicti Cantuarie situatum, presentibus tunc
ibidem prefatis venerabilibus viris magistris Cuthberto Tunstall et
Gabriele Silvester, Willelmo Potkyn et David Cooper, notariis predictis,
comparuit, coram eodem reverendissimo patre iudicialiter sedente,
Juliana Hilles uxor Roberti Hilles. Et tunc ibidem abiuravit omnes
hereses, iuxta contenta in quadam sue abiuracionis scedula eidem tunc
publice perlecta et per eandem tunc ibidem recitata, quam signo crucis
tunc ibidem manu sua signavit: prestito primitus per eandem de
peragendo penitenciam sibi per dictum reverendissimum patrem in ea
parte iniungendam, ad sancta Dei evangelia per eam corporaliter tacta,
iuramento corporali. Cuius scedule tenor sequitur videlicet.

Her abjuration. In[a] the name of God, Amen. Bifore you, the moost
reverend fader in God my lord William archibisshop of Canterbury, I,
Julian Hilles the wif of Robert Hilles of Tenterden of yor diocise of
Caunterbury, of my pure hert and free will confesse and knowlege that
I in tymes passed bifore this houre, that is to witte by the space of vi
yeres and more, have beleved, thought, said, holden, affermed and
taught of the sacraments of the churche and of the articles of the faith
otherwise than the holy church of Rome and the universall churche of
God techeth, holdeth and affermeth. And many diverse open and
damned errors and heresies contrary to the true and catholik faith and
determinacion of holy churche I have bothe secretly and openly holden,
beleved, affermed and taught. And specially among all other, these
errors and heresies folowing, that is to witte.

First, that in the sacrament of the aulter ys not the verey body of
Criste but oonly materiall bredde.

Item that goyng on pilgremages to holy and devoute places is not
meritorious nor profitable for mannys soule.

Item that worshipping off ymages of seynts is not to be doon, saying
that they be but stokks and stones.

Wherfore I, the forsaid Julyan Hilles, willing hereaftir to bileve in
the faith of Criste and of his churche and to folow the true doctryne of
holy churche, with a pure hert forsake and utterly despise my said
errors, heresies and damnable opinions and confesse them to be contrarious and repugnaunt to the faith of Criste and determinacion of his
holy churche. And therfor the said errors, heresies and opinions in

[a] Juliana Hilles *in margin.*

108

especiall and all other errors and heresies, fals doctrines and damned opinions in generall likewise contrary and repugnaunt to the faith of Criste and determinacion of his churche aforsaid I abjure, forsake and utterly renownce here bifore yor gracious lordship and all the honorable audience here assembled. And over that I swere by thies holy evangelies by me bodily here touched that from hensforth I shall never holde, teche, beleve or afferme the forsaid errors, heresies and damnable opinions nor noon other ayenst the faith of Crists holy churche and determinacion of the same. Nor yet I shall by myself or any other persone privatly or apertly defende, maynteyne, socor, favor or support any persone that to my knowlege holdeth, beleveth affer[fo. 168v]meth or techeth any suche error, heresie or damned opinions nor any persone that is suspect of the same. And if I may knowe hereaftir any persone of suche error, heresie or of any suche fals doctrines or any opinions contrary to the commen doctrine of the churche aforsaid, or if I may knowe any of their fautors, comfortors, concelors or defensors or any that have suspect books or quayers of suche errors, heresies and damned opinions, I shall without delay geve knowlege unto yor good lordship or to yor successors or to the ordinarie or ordinaries of the same persones or elles unto yor and their officers. So God me helpe and holy dome and thies holy evangelies.

In wittnes wherof to thies presents with myn owne hand I have made and subscribed the signe of the holy crosse +

Her penance. Deinde idem reverendissimus pater iniunxit eidem penitenciam infrascriptam videlicet. Quod quolibet die Veneris dum vixerit accedat ad domum sive prioratum monialium sancti Sepulchri extra muros Cantuarie[1] et ibidem dicat quinque Pater noster, v Ave et unum Credo. Et quod durante vita sua non utatur veste linea in proximiori veste, videlicet hir smokke, aliquo die Veneris de cetero. Et quod non recedat ultra suburbias dicte civitatis Cantuariensis quamdiu vixerit, nisi aliter fuerit secum dispensatum per dictum reverendissimum patrem aut suos successores.

[1] Holy Sepulchre priory of Benedictine nuns, outside the walls of Canterbury.

26. PENANCE OF ROBERT FRANKE OF TENTERDEN, 23 SEPTEMBER, 1511
[fos. 168V–169R]

His appearance in court etc. Vicesimo tercio die mensis Septembris anno Domini quo supra in ecclesia parochiali de Saltewode Cantuariensis diocesis, coram prefato reverendissimo patre pro tribunali iudicialiter sedente, presentibus tunc ibidem venerabilibus viris magistris Cuthberto Tunstall, utriusque iuris, Clemente Browne, sacre pagine, doctoribus, Johanne Aylove, in legibus bacallario, et aliis, comparuit personaliter Robertus Franke de Tenterden. Contra quem prefatus reverendissimus pater tunc ibidem tulit sentenciam. Per quam eundem Robertum perpetuis carceribus mancipandum fore decrevit et mancipavit, videlicet monasterio sancti Augustini extra muros civitatis Cantuariensis[1] et in ipsam civitatem, ita quod non recedat ab ipsis monasterio et civitate ultra unum miliare durante vita sua. Et insuper iniunxit eidem quod quolibet die Veneris coram summo altari dicti monasterii genibus flexis, more penitentis, ibidem quinquies Pater noster, quinquies Ave et unum Credo etc. Cuius sentencie tenor sequitur videlicet.

Sentence. In[a] Dei nomine, Amen. Nos, Willelmus permissione divina Cantuariensis archiepiscopus, totius Anglie primas et apostolice sedis legatus, contra te, Robertum Franke de Tenterden nostre Cantuariensis diocesis ac nostre jurisdictioni notorie subditum et subiectum, coram nobis in iudicio personaliter comparentem, ex officio nostro mero, rite et canonice procedentes.

Quia tu ex fama publica et aliis verisimilibus coniecturis nobis de et super heretica pravitate nimirum suspectus fuisti, unde iuxta iuris exigentiam purgationem canonicam ex tuis in ea parte consensu et peticione tibi indicendam fore decrevimus. In qua quidem tua purgatione huiusmodi omnino defecisti. Cuius pretextu te super huiusmodi heretica pravitate convictum invenimus.

Idcirco nos, Willelmus [fo. 169r] archiepiscopus antedictus, de consilio iurisperitorum nobis assistentium cum quibus communicavimus in hac parte, iudicialiter sedentes – abiurata per te primitus omni heretica pravitate secundum formam ecclesie consuetam, ac prestita cautione de parendo iuri et stando mandatis ecclesie ac de peragendo penitentiam per nos tibi in ea parte assignatam et assignandam – ab excommunicationis sentenciam, quam ea occasione

---

[1] St. Augustine's Abbey of Benedictine monks, outside the walls of Canterbury.

[a] Sententia contra Robertum Franke *in margin.*

incurristi, te absolvimus et sacramentis ecclesie ac communioni fidelium restituimus. In nomine Patris et Filii et Spiritus sancti, Amen. Et quia in Deum omnipotentem et sanctam ecclesiam catholicam predictis modis deliquisti, te, Robertum Franke antedictum, in monasterium sancti Augustini extra muros civitatis Cantuariensis nostre^b diocesis situatum et in dictam civitatem Cantuariensem ad perpetuam illic agendam penitentiam detrudendum esse adiudicamus et decernimus. Ita quod a dicto monasterio et civitate predicta ultra spacium unius miliaris non exeas aut recedas sed illic vita tua durante pane doloris et aqua angustie sustendandum esse volumus, decernimus et mandamus per hanc nostram sententiam diffinitivam, quam ferimus et promulgamus in his scriptis. Tibi insuper iniungentes quod, vita tua durante, quolibet die Veneris coram summo altari dicti monasterii genibus flexis, more penitentis, ibidem quinquies Pater noster, quinquies Ave Maria et unum Credo devote dicas. Reservata nobis et successoribus nostris Cantuariensibus archiepiscopis dumtaxat potestate penam sive penitentiam supradictam, si nobis aut successoribus nostris huiusmodi iustum visum fuerit, mitigandi seu alias commutandi.

Note. Et insuper monuit eundem Robertum tunc ibidem quod infra tres septimanas proxime futuras se conferat ad loca predicta ad penitentiam huiusmodi peragendam sub pena relapsus.

---

^b Cantuariensis *repeated.*

27. FORMULA OF ABSOLUTION FROM EXCOMMUNICATION, NO DATE[1]

[fo. 169R]

In[a] Dei nomine, Amen. Nos, Willelmus permissione divina
Cantuariensis archiepiscopus, totius Anglie primas et apostolice sedis
legatus, contra vos, A. B. C. D. E. F. etc., et vestrum quemlibet, in
negocio inquisitionis heretice pravitatis legitime procedentes.
Quia nobis, per confessiones vestras et vestrum cuiuslibet coram
nobis iudicialiter factas, sufficienter constat vos et quemlibet vestrum
temporibus retroactis multos et varios damnatos ac manifestos errores
et hereses credidisse, tenuisse, affirmasse et dogmatizasse: iamque, ut
asseritis, vultis ex puro corde et non ficto ad fidem catholicam, sanam
et apostolicam doctrinam et unitatem sancte matris ecclesie sponte
redire: attendentesque quod sancta mater ecclesia nullo claudit
gremium redire volenti et quod Deus non vult mortem peccatoris sed ut
magis convertatur et vivat: abiurata per vos et vestrum quemlibet omni
heretica pravitate, ac prestita etiam per vos et quemlibet vestrum
cautione de parendo iuri et stando mandatis ecclesie ac iniunctionibus
nostris vobis et cuilibet vestrum occasione premissorum faciendis, et
penitentiam per nos vobis et vestrum ut prefertur cuilibet in hac parte
assignandam fideliter perimplendo: ab excommunicationis sententia,
quam ea occasione incurristis et vestrum quilibet incurrit, vos ac
vestrum quemlibet absolvimus et sacramentis ecclesie et communioni
fidelium restituimus. In nomine Patris et Filii et Spiritus sancti, Amen.

---

[1] This section follows in Warham's register after section 26, which is dated 23
September, 1511 (see above, 110).

[a] Absolutio abiuratorum *in margin.*

112

28. PENANCE OF WILLIAM PELLAND OF TENTERDEN, 17 DECEMBER, 1511
[fo. 175V]

Sentence. In[a] Dei nomine, Amen. Nos, Robertus Wodewarde, decretorum doctor, reverendissimi in Christo patris et domini, domini Willelmi permissione divina Cantuariensis archiepiscopi, totius Anglie primatis et apostolice sedis legati, in suis civitate et diocesi Cantuariensibus commissarius generalis, contra te, Willelmum Pelland de Tenterden Cantuariensis diocesis ac nostre iurisdictionis notorie subditum et subiectum, coram nobis in iudicio personaliter comparentem, ex officio nostro mero, rite et canonice procedentes.

Quia tu ex fama publica et aliis verisimilibus coniecturis nobis de et super heretica pravitate nimirum suspectus fuisti, unde iuxta iuris exigentiam purgationem canonicam ex tuis in hac parte consensu et petitione tibi indicendam fore decrevimus. In qua quidem tua purgatione huiusmodi omnino defecisti. Cuius pretextu te super huiusmodi heretica pravitate convictum invenimus.

Idcirco nos, Robertus commissarius antedictus, de concilio iurisperitorum nobis assistencium cum quibus communicavimus in hac parte pro tribunali iudicialiter sedentibus – abiurata per[b] te primitus omni heretica pravitate secundum formam ecclesie consuetam, ac prestita cautione de parendo iuri et stando mandatis ecclesie ac de peragendo penitenciam per nos tibi in hac parte assignatam et assignandam – ab excommunicacionis sentencia, quam ea occasione incurristi, te absolvimus et sacramentis ecclesie ac communioni fidelium restituimus. In nomine Patris et Filii et Spiritus sancti, Amen.

Et quia in Deum omnipotentem et sanctam ecclesiam catholicam predictis modis deliquisti, te, Willelmum Pelland, in monasterium de Boxley[1] Cantuariensis diocesis ad perpetuam illic peragendam penitenciam detrudendum esse adiudicamus et decernimus. Itaque a dicto monasterio ultra spacium duorum miliarium non exeas aut recedas. Sed illic tua vita durante pane doloris et aqua angustie sustentandum esse volumus, decernimus et mandamus per hanc nostram sentenciam diffinitivam, quam ferimus et promulgamus in hiis scriptis. Tibi insuper iniungentes quod, vita tua durante, quolibet die Veneris coram summo altari dicti monasterii genibus flexis, more penitentis, ibidem quinquies Pater noster, Ave Maria et unum Credo devote dicas. Reservata prefato reverendissimo patri et suis successoribus Cantuariensibus archiepiscopis dumtaxat potestate penam sive

---

[1] The abbey of Cistercian monks at Boxley, Kent.

---

[a] Sentenciam (*sic*) contra Pelland *in margin.*   [b] *MS.* par.

penitenciam supradictam, si eidem reverendissimo patri archiepiscopo et suis successoribus huiusmodi iustum visum fuerit, mitigandi seu alias commutandi +

Note. Xvii[mo] die mensis Decembris anno Domini millesimo quingentesimo undecimo in ecclesia Christi Cantuariense[2] lecta fuit per dominum commissarium etc., presentibus tunc et ibidem.

[2] Canterbury Cathedral.

29. PENANCE OF JULIAN HILLES OF TENTERDEN, NO DATE[1] [fo. 175V]

Te, Julianam Hilles de Tenterden etc., in prioratum domus sancti Sepulcri etc.[2] ultram spacium duorum miliarium.

[1] This section follows in Warham's register after section 28, which is dated 17 December, 1511 (see above, 114). The wording follows, in abbreviated form, a paragraph of the sentences of perpetual imprisonment (see above 00 and elsewhere), so Julian Hilles is probably being sentenced to imprisonment.

[2] See above, 109, note 1.

115

30. ABJURATIONS AND/OR PENANCES OF JOHN AND JOAN BUKHERST, JOAN
AND JOHN DODDE, JOHN AND RABAGE BENET, ALL OF STAPLEHURST,
5 JUNE, 1512 [fos. 167R–167*R]

Heading. Abiurationes facte anno Domini millesimo quingentesimo
duodecimo, coram dicto reverendissimo patre, sequuntur.

Appearance in court etc. Quinto die mensis Junii anno Domini millesimo
quingentesimo duodecimo in capella reverendissimi patris et domini,
domini Willelmi permissione divina Cantuariensis archiepiscopi, predicta
de Knoll, coram eodem reverendissimo patre pro tribunali iudicialiter
sedente, assidentibus eidem magistris Cuthberto Tunstall, eius cancellario,
Gilberto^a Silvester, Thoma Welles et Clemente Browne, sacre theologie
professoribus, Johanne Aylove et Ingilrano Bedill,[1] eiusdem
reverendissimi patris capellanis, in etiam Willelmo Potkyn et David
Cooper, notariorum publicorum, presentia, comparuerunt personaliter
Johannes Bukherst, Johanna Dodde, Johannes Benet et Rabage Benett,
eius uxor, de Stapleherst Cantuariensis diocesis. Qui omnes et singuli tunc
ibidem abiurarunt omnes et singulos hereses, errores et damnatas
opiniones in quibus [fo. 167v] fatebantur se tunc ibidem errasse contra
catholicam fidem et ecclesie universalis determinactionem in specie, ac
omnes alios hereses et errores in ea parte in genere, iuxta et secundum
contenta in scedulis abiurationum suarum huiusmodi eis et eorum cuilibet
publice perlectis et per eosdem de verbo ad verbum recitatis ac signo
crucis manibus eorum consignatis: prestito primitus per eosdem de
peragendo penitentiam, per dictum reverendissimum patrem eis in ea
parte iniungendam, iuramento corporali. Quarum scedularum tenores
sequuntur videlicet.

Abjuration of John Bukherst. In^b the name of God, Amen. Bifore you,
the moost reverend fader in God my lord William archibisshop of
Caunterbury, I, John Bukherst of Stapleherst of your diocise of
Caunterbury, of my pure hert and free will confesse and knowlege that
[I] in tymes passed bifore this houre, that is to witte by the space of xii
yeres and more, have beleved, thought, said, holden, affermed and
taught of the sacraments of the churche and of the articules of the faith
otherwise than the holy church of Rome and universall churche of God
techeth, holdeth and observeth. And many divers, open and damned
errors and heresies contrary to the true and catholike faith and

---

[1] See *BRUO*, i, 148, Ingram Bedyll.

^a *Sic, presumably an error for* Gabriele.   ^b Johannes Bukherst *in margin.*

determinacion of holy churche I have bothe secretly and openly holden and beleved, affermed and taught. And specially among all other, thies errors and heresies folowing, that is to witte.

First, that the sacrament of the aulter was not the verey body of Crist but oonly brede.

Also that a prest hadde no more power than a layman to mynistre any sacrament of holy churche.

Also that images of the crucifixe, our Lady and of other seynts were not to be worshipped.

Also that pilgremage was not necessary to be doon.

Also that holy brede and holy water were no better for the benediccion doon by the preest than they were bifore.

Also that Crist was not incarnatt nor borne of our lady the virgin Mary, nor deed suffer passion for the redempcion of mannys soule, nor dide aryse from deth to lyve the third day aftir his passion.

Wherfore I, the forsaid John Bukherst, willing hereaftir to beleve in the faith of Crist and of his churche and to folow the true doctrine of holy churche, with a pure hert forsake and utterly despise my said errors, heresies and damnable opinions and confesse theym to be contrarius and repugnaunt to the faith of Criste and determinacion of his holy churche. And therfore the said errors, heresies and opinions in especiall and all other errors, heresies, fals doctrines and damned opinions in generall likewise contrary and repugnaunt to the faith of Crist and determinacion of his church aforesaid I abjure, forsake and utterly renownce here bifore yor gracious lordship and all the honorable audience here assembled. And over that I swere by thies holy evaungelies by me bodily here touched that from hensforth I shall never holde, teche, beleve or afferme the said errors, heresies and damnable opinions nor noon other ayenst the faith of Crists holy churche and determinacion of the same. Nor yet I shall by myself or any other persone privatly or apertly defende, maynteyne, socor, favor or support any persone that to my knowlege holdeth, beleveth, affermeth or techeth any suche error, heresie or damned opinions nor any persone that is suspected of the same. And if I may knowe hereaftir any persone of suche error, heresie or of any suche fals doctrine or any opinions contrary to the commen doctrine of the church aforesaid, or if I may know any of their fautors, comfortors, concelors or defensors or any that have suspect books or quayers of suche errors, heresies or damend opinions, I shall withoute delay geve knowlege unto yor goode lordship or to yor successors or to the ordinarie or ordinaries of the same persones or elles unto yor and their officers. So God me helpe and holy doom and thies holy evaungelies.

In wittnes wherof to thies presents with myn owne hand I have made and subscribed the signe of the holy crosse. + John Bukherst

Abjuration of Joan Dodde. In[c] the name of God, Amen. Bifore you, the most reverend fader in God my lord William archibisshop of Caunterbury, I, Johanne Dodde, the wif of John Dodde, flecher, of yor diocese of Canterbury, of my pure hert and free will confesse and knowlege that I in tymes passed bifore this howre, that is to witte by the space of half yere last passed and more, have beleved, thought, said, holden, affermed and taught of the sacraments of the churche and of the articles of the faith otherwise than the holy churche of Rome and universall church of God techeth, holdeth and observeth. And many and divers open and damned errors and heresies contrary to the true and catholike faith and determinacion of holy churche I have bothe secretly and openly holden, beleved, affermed and taught. And specially among other, this error and heresie folowing, that is to witte.

That the sacrament of the aulter was not the verey body of Crist but oonly bredde.

Wherfore I, the forsaid Johanne Dodde, willing hereaftir to beleve in the faith of Criste and of his church and to folowe the true doctrine of holy churche, with a pure hert forsake and utterly despise my said error, heresies[d] and damnable opinion and confesse theym to be contrarius and repugnaunt to the faith of Crist and determinacion of his holy churche. And therfore the said error, heresies and opinion in especiall and all other errors, heresies, fals doctrines and damned opinions in generall likewise contrary and repugnaunt to the faith of Criste and determinacion of his churche aforsaid I abjure, forsake and utterly renownce here bifore yor gracious lordship and all the honorable audience here assembled. And over that I swere by thies holy evaungelies by me bodily here touched that from hensforth I shall never holde, teche, bileve or afferme the foresaide errors, heresies and damnable opinions nor noon other ayenst the faith of Criste, holy churche and determinacion of the same. Nor yet I shall by myself or any other persone privately or apertly defende, maynteyn, socor, favor or supporte any persone that to my knowlege holdeth, beleveth, affermeth or techeth any suche error, heresie or damned opinion nor any persone that is suspect of the same. And if I may knowe hereaftir any persone of suche error, heresie or of any suche fals doctrines or any opinions contrary to the commen doctrine of the church aforsaid, or if I may know any off their fautors, comfortors, concelors or defensors or any that have suspect books or quayers of suche errors, heresies or damned opinions, I shall withoute delay geve knowlege unto yor good lordship or to yor successors or to the ordinarie or ordinaries of the

---

[c] Johanna Dodde *in margin.*
[d] *Sic, singular and plural alternating here and in the rest of this and the two following abjurations.*

118

same persones or elles unto yor and their officers. So God me helpe and holy dome and thies holy evaungelies.

In wittnes wherof to these present with myn owne hand I have made and subscribed the signe of the holy crosse. + Johanne Dodde

Abjuration of John Benet. In^e the name of God, Amen. Bifore you, the most reverend fader in God my lord William archiebisshop of Caunterbury, I, John Benet of Stapleherst of yor diocise of Canterbury, of my pure here and free will confesse and knowlege that I in tymes passed bifore this houre, that is to witte by the space of ii yeres and more, have beleved, thought, said, holden, affermed and taught of the sacraments of the churche and of the articles of the feith [otherwise] than the holy churche of Rome and universall churche of God techeth, holdeth and observeth. And many divers open and damned errors and heresies contrary to the true and catholik faith and determinacion of holy churche I have bothe secretly and openly holden and bileved, affermed and taught. And specially among all other, thies error and heresies folowing, that is to witte.

That the sacrament of the aulter was not the verey body of Crist butt oonly bredde.

Wherfore I, the forsaid John Benett, willing hereaftir to bileve in the faith of Criste and of his churche and to folow the true doctrine of holy churche, with a pure hert forsake and utterly despise my said error, heresies and damnable opinion and confesse them to be contraryous and repugnaunt to the faith of Crist and determinacion of his holy churche. And therfore the said error, heresies and opinion in especiall and all other errors and heresies, fals doctrines and damned opinions in generall likewise contrary and repugnaunt to the faith of Crist and determinacion of his church aforesaid I abjure, forsake and utterly renownce here bifore yor gracious lordship and all the honorable audience [fo. 167*r] here assembled. And over that I swere by thies holy evaungelies by me bodily here touched that from hensforth I shall never holde, teche, beleve or afferme the forsaid errors, heresies and damnable opinions nor noon other ayenst the faith of Crists holy churche and determinacion of the same. Nor yet I shall by myself or any other persone pryvately or apertly defende, maynteyn, socour, favor or support any persone that to my knowlege holdeth, beleveth, affermeth or techeth any suche error, heresie or damned opinions nor any persone that ys suspect of the same. And if I may knowe hereaftir any persone of suche error, heresie or of any suche false doctrines or any opinions contrary to the commen doctrine of the churche aforsaid, or if I may know any of their fautors,

---

^e Johannes Benet *in margin.*

comfortors, concelors or defensors or any that have suspect books or
quayers of suche errors, heresies or damned opinions, I shall withoute
delay geve knowlege unto yor goode lordship or to yor successors or to
the ordinarie or ordinaries of the same persones or elles unto yor and
their officers. So God me helpe and holy dome and thies holy
evaungelies.

In wittnes wherof to thies presents with myn owne hand I have and
subscribed the signe of the holy crosse. + John Benet

Abjuration of Rabage Benet. In[f] the name of God, Amen. Byfore you,
the most reverend fader in God my lord William archibisshop of
Caunterbury, I, Rabeche Benet the wif of John Benet of yor diocise of
Caunterbury, of my pure hert and free will confesse and knowlege that
in tymes passed bifore this howre, that is to witte by the space of xxiii
yeres and more, have beleved, thought, said, holden, affermed and
taught of the sacraments of the churche and of the articles of the faith
otherwise than the holy church of Rome and universall church of God
techeth, holdeth and observeth. And many diverse open and damned
errors and heresies contrary to the true and catholik faith and
determinacion of holy churche I have bothe secretly and openly holden
and beleved, affermed and taught. And specially among all other, thies
errors and heresies folowing, that is to witte.

That the sacrament of the aulter was not the verey body of Criste but
oonly bredde.

Wherfore I, the forsaid Rabache Benett, willing heraftir to beleve in
the faith of Criste and of his churche and to folowe the true doctrine of
holy churche, with a pure hert forsake and utterly despise my said error,
heresies and damnable opinions and confesse theym to be contrarius
and repugnaunt to the faith of Criste and determinacion of his holy
church. And therfore the said error, heresies and opinions in especiall
and all other errors and heresies, fals doctrines and damned opinions in
generall likewise contrary and repugnaunt to the faith of Crist and
determinacion of his churche aforsaid I abjure, forsake and utterly
renownce here bifore yor gracious lordship and all the honorable
audience here assembled. And over that I swere by thies hooly
evaungelies by me bodily here touched that from hensforth I shall
never holde, teche, beleve or afferme the forsaid error, heresies and
damnable opinions nor noon other ayenst the faith of Crists holy
churche and determinacion of the same. Nor yet I shall by myself or
any other persone privately or apertly defende, maynteyn, socor, favor
or support any persone that to my knowlege holdeth, beleveth,

[f] Rabage Benett *in margin.*

affermeth or techeth any suche error, heresie or damned opinion nor any persons that is suspect of the same. And if I may knowe hereaftir any persone of suche errour, heresie or of any suche fals doctrines or any opinions contrary to the commen doctrine of the churche aforesaid, or if I may knowe any of their fautors, comfortors, concelors or defensors or any that have suspect books or quayers of suche errors, heresies or damned opinions I shall withoute delay geve knowlege unto yor goode lordship or to yor successors or to the ordinaries or ordinarie of the same persones or elles unto yor or their officers. So God me helpe and holy dome and thies holy evaungelies.

In wittnes wherof to the presents with myn owne hand I have made and subscribed the signe of the holy crosse. + Rabage Benet

Penances of John Bukherst and John Benet. Insuper tunc ibidem idem reverendissimus pater iniunxit dicto Johanni Bukherst et Johanni Benet quod antecedant processionem circa ecclesiam parochialem de Stapleherst predict' – nudi capita tibias et pedes – die corporis [Christi],[2] gestantes fasciculum ligneum in humeris suis. Et post processionem stabunt in medio dicte ecclesie ante chorum eiusdem, gestantes idem fasciculum usque ad finem magne misse. Et post magnam missam huiusmodi fasciculum in porticu ecclesie ibidem relinquent. Et similem peragent penitenciam duabus diebus Dominicis proxime ex tunc sequentibus in eadem ecclesia.

Item quod non amovebunt se a loco ubi iam inhabitant, nisi certificato dicto reverendissimo patre de loco ubi inhabitare intendunt.

Penances of Joan Dodde and Rabage Benet. Etiam idem reverendissimus pater iniunxit Johanne Dodde et Rabage Benet quod die corporis Christi proxime futuro circa ecclesiam parochialem de Stapleherst predictam antecedant processionem – nude tibias et pedes – gestantes fascicula lignea in humeris suis. Et post processionem huiusmodi fascicula ibidem ad gradum ostii chori deponent, et ibidem genuflectent usque post missam magnam ibidem finitam. Et eodem die offerent, et earum quelibet offeret, unum denarium ad summum altare tempore misse huiusmodi. Et consimilem paragent penitenciam die Dominica proxime ex tunc sequente in eadem ecclesia de Stapleherst.

Oath and penance of John Dodde. Eisdem die et loco prefatus reverendissimus pater iurare fecit Johannem Dodde de fideliter peragendo penitentiam sibi iniungendam, eo quod concelavit certas hereses. Qui sic ad sancta Dei evangelia, per eum corporaliter tacta, iuravit.

---

[2] The feast of Corpus Christi was kept on 10 June in 1512.

Et^g deinde idem reverendissimus pater iniunxit eidem quod die Veneris proximo ibit – nudus caput tibias et pedes – et offeret unum cereum valoris unius denarii coram imagine beate Marie virginis in ecclesia parochiale de Stapleherst. Et similem penitentiam peraget die Veneris proxime ex tunc sequente. Et quod ex nunc bene et honeste tractabit uxorem suam. Et eundem sic dimisit.

Penance of Joan Bukherst. Item^h dictis die et loco idem reverendissimus pater iniunxit Johanne Bukherst, uxori Johannis Bukherst superius nominati, eo quod concelavit opiniones mariti sui, quod non comedet pisces quinque diebus Veneris proxime futuris.

31. DISMISSAL OF JAMES BUKHERST, 5 JUNE, 1512 [fo. 167*R]

Etiam[a] dictis die et loco prefatus reverendissimus pater[1] dimisit Jacobum Bukherst, non convictum, non confessum, ab ulteriore comparitione etc.

---

[1] For the date, place and *reverendissimus pater*, see above, 116.

[a] Dimissio Jacobi Bukherst *in margin.*

32. OATH OF WILLIAM BUKHERST, 28 JUNE, 1512 [fo. 167*R-V]

Vicesimo octavo die mensis Juni anno Domini millesimo quingentesimo duodecimo in loco registrali prerogative Lamehith,[1] coram magistro Cuthberto Tunstall, prefati reverendissimi patris et domini, domini Willelmi permissione divina Cantuariensis archiepiscopi, totius Anglie primatus et apostolice sedis legati, cancellario, comparuit personaliter Willelmus [fo. 167*v][a] Bukherst, shomaker, et promisit ac iuramentum corporale prestitit de sistendo seipsum coram dicto reverendissimo patre quandocunque fuerit ad hoc vocatus auctore eiusdem reverendissimi patris.

---

[1] The registry within the archbishop's manor at Lambeth (see Churchill, *Canterbury Administration*, i, 421).

[a] personaliter Willelmus *repeated as first words on fo. 167*v*.

GENERAL INDEX

All the places are in Kent unless indicated otherwise. For variant spellings of the places in Kent, see underneath the Map, above xxvi.